Kat Kerr   Stephanie SKidd Adams

'This is a wonderful book … f … finishing well with grea … … wholeheartedly recommen … today.'
Gavin Calver, Director of M … Spring Harvest Planning Grou,

'This is a brilliant book. Miroslav Volf and Rio Ferdinand rub shoulders with Martin Luther King and Leonard Cohen as Ann Clifford explores every bit of the landscape of The Thing We Never Talk About. Loads of God-soaked wisdom and spiritual insight about death – the journey, the emotions and the realities. And heaps of practical advice about making a will, caring for those left behind, and dying well. It's the book we all need as we face the death of loved ones and our own mortality.'
Pete Broadbent, Bishop of Willesden & Acting Bishop of London

'This is a very human book, which deals without flinching with one of the most difficult questions of human life – how do we come to terms with death. Full of compassionate and personal stories, the book offers gentle and whimsical insights into how we can overcome our reluctance to face the inevitable. Ann Clifford is neither unrealistic nor morbid but leads her readers with understanding and empathy through those crucial issues we so often avoid, never forgetting the impact also on our loved ones. She offers help in facing fear without platitudes, and the future with care and planning, while encouraging us in the hope of life beyond the grave. The second half of the book on practicalities is a goldmine of carefully sifted information where legal, financial and institutional issues are unpacked with ease and difficult terms are explained and explored. The result is a book that reaches out and instils confidence in our human significance at every stage of our lives.'
Elaine Storkey, theologian and author of Scars Across Humanity

'This book flows out of the compassion Ann has for people. She writes about the event we will all face one day in a way that is accessible, innovative, inspiring and practical. Her honesty and deep Christian faith provide a credibility that will attract many readers.'
Elfed Godding, Director of Coalitions and Wales, Evangelical Alliance

'This is a brave book. It steps into a subject matter that most of us are desperate to ignore, and yet the message of this book is that to ignore it is a mistake. We should prepare and have in place both the practical and the relational legacies that are dear and important to us. Death will knock on every door with absolute certainty. *Time to Live* will in a strange way inspire us and equip us to face that day. I highly recommend it; it is beautifully written and it will move your heart.'
Laurence Singlehurst, Director of Cell UK, author, Chair of Board of Trustees at Westminster Theological Centre

'I congratulate Ann on dealing with this subject of death so sensitively and warmly, despite it being such a taboo subject to speak about openly. *Time to Live* is an excellent resource, with many helpful and practical suggestions and tools on how to deal with the difficult and emotive issue of death.'
Ram Gidoomal CBE, Chair, Stewardship Services and The Lausanne Movement

'Beautifully written, Ann's book offers us a companion through the huge practical and emotional challenges and opportunities of facing death well. It will enrich and uplift you through what conspires to sap you of life. Please have the courage to read it.'
Maggie Ellis, Executive Coach and Psychotherapist

'I praise God for giving the vision to Ann Clifford to write this book and I honour Ann for her obedience. To know life is to know death. Thank you, Ann, for having the courage to write about the things most people don't want to talk about. You have put words to feelings and held nothing back. For your honesty, bravery and transparency, I am so grateful. This book is informative and personal and at the same time practical.'

Pastor Chrishanthy Sathiyaraj, Bethany Church Southall, One People Commission, EA Council member

'Ann Clifford has produced a little gem of a book. Creative and compassionate, poetic and practical. It is full of inspiring stories and Spirit filled wisdom. I wish it had been available when I led a church – I can think of so many people who would have benefited greatly from reading it.'

Dr Fred Drummond, Director of Prayer, Evangelical Alliance

'*Time to Live* is extraordinary in its content and unusual in its mix of being beautifully written, life enhancing and yet very, very practical. I have found myself moved to tears, inspired to die well and provided with a practical list of ideas I want to implement right now.

'Reading this book will draw out of you a desire to be brave, to be considerate and to be full of future hope. The desire to be brave will come as you are provoked to look the inevitability of death in the face, to talk about it and to prepare for it. The desire to be considerate to those you love the most will come as you are challenged to ensure all is left in order when you die, from funeral arrangements to financial arrangements. The desire to be a person full of future hope will come as you gain a clear and beautiful vision of heaven.

'*Time to Live* reframes death entirely, to the extent that after reading it, you might consider that the day you die will actually be the best day of your life so far. With that perspective in mind, you can truly and deeply live.'

Ness Wilson, Team Leader of Open Heaven Church

TIME TO LIVE

The Beginner's Guide to Saying Goodbye

It is not about the preservation of our body, but our spirit/personality/essence becoming more like Him, the One we long to meet face to face.

Pg 63

Ann Clifford

instant
apostle

First published in Great Britain in 2017

Instant Apostle
The Barn
1 Watford House Lane
Watford
Herts
WD17 1BJ

British Library Cataloguing-in-Publication Data

A catalogue record for this book is available from the British Library

This book and all other Instant Apostle books are available from Instant Apostle:

Website: www.instantapostle.com
E-mail: info@instantapostle.com

ISBN 978 1 909728 68 4

Printed in Great Britain

To Steve, Jake, Asha, Judah, Jordan and Stuart
You have my heart – always

Acknowledgements

This book would not have been possible without a great deal of help.

Simon Cox, who encouraged me to write it in the first place.

My sisters, Carol and Lucy, unwavering in their support together with the rest of my family.

Patrick Dixon, who helped me keep going.

The many kindnesses of those who listened to my questions and gave me their expertise; they should find themselves credited in the footnotes.

Thanks to all those who gave me permission for quotations.

Paul McGoun, Simon Hassan, Maddy Thomson, Katrina Moss; my book club; my West London Writers' Group; Jill from my dance class; my editor, Sheila Jacobs; my publisher; and finally, my friends, who cheer me on.

Thank you all.

Contents

Foreword by Dr Patrick Dixon 15

Introduction 17

PART ONE: JOURNEY 19

Chapter 1: We Are Human 21

Chapter 2: Facing Our Fears 55

Chapter 3: Our Future 83

Chapter 4: Emotional Health – Communicating with
Ourselves and Our Loved Ones 97

Chapter 5: Counselling/Guidance 121

PART TWO: PRACTICALITIES 131

Chapter 6: Leaving with Order 133

Finale 191

APPENDIX 1: To-do list when someone dies 199

APPENDIX 2: Choosing a care home or nursing home 209

APPENDIX 3: Visiting activities 213

Resources 217

Foreword

This is a really important, unique and beautifully crafted book which will enrich your life: full of passion, compassion and common sense about living and about dying. Packed with vivid and often moving personal stories, and faithful reflections, it has an almost poetic style on every page, and every chapter breathes hope and wholeness.

As a hospice-trained doctor, I have had the privilege of being with many people in the last few weeks of their journey of physical life, and I have learned so much, laughed a lot and wept many times. Ann shows us why it is that so many of us only start becoming in some ways fully alive when confronted by the real possibility that soon our physical lives may be coming to an end.

The final sections are a vital guide to the practicalities like planning a funeral or making a will, and bring clarity to things such as Advanced Directives or planning your future medical treatment. Ann asks profound questions and brings deep insight as well as spiritual revelation. Above all, Ann points us forward and upward to another tomorrow: to Life beyond life, and to the ultimate significance of every unique human being.

Dr Patrick Dixon, Chair, Global Change Ltd
28th February 2017

Introduction

As I write this introduction, my son and my daughter-in-law sit beside their premature baby in the neo-natal unit, having been thrown into parenthood at the deep end. Their beautiful little son, my grandson, was seven weeks premature and, while he is fully formed with everything functioning, he is a mere 2.5lbs. His journey has already contained highs and lows. He needs to learn to suckle to enable him to gain weight more effectively. My son and his wife live temporarily in a charmless parents' room in the hospital. The baby is four days old, and it is excruciating to write this book at the same time. The deadline for my first draft to the editor is less than four weeks away. It is at times such as this, when your children are in pain, you ask yourself, where is God?

I find myself praying a lot and wishing I knew how to do it better. I want to immerse myself in this God I have followed for many years, curl up in a ball, and know everything will be all right. The truth is, there are no guarantees. My choice, and the choice of my son and his wife, is, will we allow God to be free? To be the God who revealed Himself in Jesus as an extravagantly generous, supernatural human being. Someone who loved to love every single person He met, whether they returned that love or not. A humble working man, who gave everything He had, including His life, for you, for me, for my son, his wife and their tiny son. Will we allow God to be Lord of all things, or will we insist He only does what we permit? If we do that, then we cut God down to our size; we limit His power; we worship not God, but an image of ourselves.

This God embodied as Jesus, who as a human being was extraordinary... Yet when His followers met Him after the resurrection, He told them it was better that He left because only then could they meet the Comforter. This Comforter, this Holy Spirit, would help them in all things. This Comforter would never leave them. This Comforter would bring them sustenance every moment of every day, should they wish it.

As I bring these words to you, I trust within them you will find a friendly voice to walk with you on your journey. I hope you will allow the Comforter to accompany you as you travel. Whatever your story, I know it is singularly important to God. You are known by name and you are loved.

My son finds the thought of his son alone in the incubator distressing. I reassure him. He is not alone. None of us is alone. The Comforter is present. It is promised that if we look for Him, we will find Him.[1]

---

[1] 'When you come looking for me, you'll find me' (Jeremiah 29:13, *The Message*).

PART ONE

JOURNEY

Chapter 1
We Are Human

There is no getting away from it. We are all going to die.

We have so many words and ways to avoid this truth and the word 'death'. No one has ever expressed death with more humour than Monty Python. Along with millions, I loved the 'Dead Parrot' sketch.[2]

We say things such as fell asleep, bit the dust, popped their clogs, cashed in their chips, gone to a better place, passed away, shuffled off the mortal coil, slipped away, called home, at peace, joined the choir invisible. I'm sure you can think of many others.

This is a difficult and challenging arena to reflect on. Dying hits at the core of our being and most of us do not want to contemplate the possibility, let alone talk with others. We find it difficult to find something positive to say because in today's society death is the worst thing that can happen to us. We have harnessed millions of pounds, vast technology, incredible scientific progress, stunning medical understanding to keep us alive for as long as possible. However, there is no invention to stop us from dying.

---

[2] Monty Python,' Dead Parrot', *Monty Python's Flying Circus*, Season 1, Episode 8.

A new term to me is 'Transhumanism'. It is based on the idea that death happens and we need to address it as a technical/scientific problem to be solved. There is a group of people devoting themselves to finding the solution. They address the possibility of eternal life, but one that is man-made. To me this expresses the ultimate fear of death.

What started this journey was an initiative which I began about six years ago. We called it Tea-Timers and it was a free tea, including freshly made sandwiches and cakes, for the elderly. We collected proper china tea services from charity shops because we determined it would be a life-enhancing experience – a treat for all our guests. We also wanted it to endure, to be something we could invest a number of years in. So we concluded that a monthly celebration, while not much, would guarantee longevity. What I didn't allow for was the fact that I would fall in love with such a variety of people.

Some of our guests have since died. As I experienced this, went to a funeral, I longed for a tool to help us all talk about dying and death, whether people had faith or not.

As I face death head on, and for my family and loved ones, I want them to let me go as I allow myself to let them go. I want to leave them peaceful and thankful for all the time we had, not churned up, living in pain because I let them down and didn't die well. Writing this book has convinced me that we need to think about how we will say goodbye. I regard this as a process. It cannot be a single moment. We owe it to those we love, to help them to open their eyes too and prepare for what is the inevitable for every single one of us.

When I gaze at myself in the mirror, I see a person who is ageing. I don't like it, I don't want it, but it is happening. I do not want to try to appear younger, I do not want to pretend or hide from the truth. I want to be me, a me at peace at every stage of my life. As I considered how I would tackle this, a God-lover of many years, I found this quotation by Eugene Peterson. When I read these words from his wonderful and inspiring book about the prophet Jeremiah, my heart leapt.

> We do not deteriorate. We do not disintegrate. We become.
> *Eugene H. Peterson*[3]

Peterson, in these words, expresses the inspiring truth that if we are God-lovers, then we are on the journey of 'becoming'. This journey then becomes not about what I perceive I am losing, rather about gaining what I have spent my life pursuing. This can be true for every single person who is reading this book.

> But friends, that's exactly who we are: children of God. And that's only the beginning. Who knows how we'll end up! What we know is that when Christ is openly revealed, we'll see him – and in seeing him, become like him.
> *1 John 3:2 (The Message)*

Let us journey together. My context is that of faith in the God of the Judaeo–Christian Bible. Let's dare to explore

---

[3] Eugene H. Peterson, *Run with the Horses* (Downers Grove, IL: IVP, 2010).

together the often fear-inducing, let's-ignore-for-as-long-as-possible reality of our physical mortality. While our bodies may deteriorate and disintegrate, something far more wonderful can happen to us. We can work with God and become more like the One we love, the One we serve, the One who created us. At the moment of our death, when we leave our earthbound body, we will fulfil our heart's desire and see Him. When we return with Him, we shall 'become' who we were born to be in the fullest sense possible.

> And we, who with unveiled faces all reflect the Lord's glory, are being transformed into his likeness with ever-increasing glory, which comes from the Lord, who is the Spirit.
> *2 Corinthians 3:18*

We get glimpses of this glory in the lives of believers. Yet there will be more.

My God is the one who took on human flesh, lived, died and rose again for us. The God who loves not only us, but every single human being on this earth, without measure. That includes everyone who reads this book. You are loved.

I am interested that 'become' means 'begin to be'. We began as a baby in our mother's womb. We continued in our 'being' as we grew into our human life. Our instincts tell many of us there is more to 'being' than mere physicality. As Charles Taylor[4] comments, the 'ghost of

---

[4] James K. A. Smith, *How (Not) to Be Secular: Reading Charles Taylor* (Grand Rapids, MI: Eerdmans, 2014).

transcendence' haunts many of us. The sense that 'there must be more to life than this'. Many of us then travel earnest and honest in our journey to discover a relevant spirituality.

The Bible hints at what this becoming means. Our lives hint at what this becoming means. Yet the ultimate fullness of the meaning remains a mystery because it remains unimaginable to our human minds. When I die, I expect the mystery to unfold into something altogether wonderful.

We are beginners at dying. To tackle the absolute inevitability of my death I craved a vision of what I will become when I leave this physical world. The notion of 'becoming more like him'[5] delights and excites me in my day-to-day living. The notion of that being fulfilled in my dying, my resurrection and new life in a new heaven and a new earth, fills me with courage and hope.　　　　✳

Only one person has risen from the dead and illustrated resurrection. It is that person I choose to follow.　*Matthew 10:8*

If you picked up, opened and started this book, then you have perhaps found yourself in a difficult and demanding place. I am so sorry. There are many challenges for each of us on our life journey, but facing our own death, or the death of a precious loved one, is without doubt the most arduous.

Maybe you have selected this book because you are brave. You want to explore what most shy away from. I congratulate you.

Heal the sick,
raise the dead
cleanse those who have leprosy
drive out demons

---

[5] 2 Corinthians 3:18 (ISV).

25

May we become empowered, envisioned and emboldened together on this journey.

The planted seed

The Bible is full of pictures.

A seed[6] planted into the ground to germinate carries within it a sense of promise, a sense of excitement as we wait for the metamorphosis from dormancy into a growing, living plant. Seeds present as if they are dead. For a designated time they disappear into the earth. Given the right conditions it is only a matter of time before something beautiful occurs.

An emotive metaphor for dying.

We will leave our mortal bodies and we too will experience metamorphosis; we will 'become'.

So what if ...?

- What if dying carried with it a sense of promise and a sense of excitement?

- What if meditating about dying brought a fresh sense of perspective and purpose?

- What if talking about dying, although scary, was positive and helpful not only for ourselves, but also for those whom we love?

- What if we took the opportunity to finish our life well, perhaps in contrast to some other life decisions?

---

[6] The parable of the seeds, Mark 4:3ff.

- What if we could resolve what remains unresolved in our lives to the best of our abilities?

- What if we could be brave and courageous about death and leave a positive and healthy legacy?

- What if we were to face the unthinkable and discover peace?

- What if, in our dying and death, we became our best selves?

These are exciting thoughts. Don't get me wrong. I am not eager to die. I am married. I love my husband even though we have been together for aeons. I adore my two grown-up married children and their partners. Their lives are rich and interesting. Babies are being born. We love all being together. Whenever we are together at the same time I raid the supermarket, I kill the 'fatted calf'. We celebrate because life can be magnificent, and being together is one of life's greatest joys.

Allow me a moment to digress – in life let's all celebrate more. It's fun and life-enhancing. Great forever memories.

What do you love? What do you live for? I don't live for my work although I love writing. Nor for the plaudits of my next accomplishment. Although I always welcome the occasional plaudit, if I am honest!

I live for relationship.

My core relationship is my relationship with the One God – Father, Son and Holy Spirit; then that with my family. But I am part of a whole family which is much bigger than my nuclear family. They are precious, and when I celebrate, I include as many of my church family and neighbourhood friends as possible. I am blessed by God and I like to share it.

Life happens. It is difficult, painful, joyous, terrible, exciting, troublesome, frustrating, amazing, shocking, tragic, any number of adjectives, and people die. We all need an anchor. Where is yours?

> 'Do not let your hearts be troubled. Trust in God; trust also in me. In my Father's house are many rooms; if it were not so, I would have told you. I am going there to prepare a place for you. And if I go and prepare a place for you, I will come back and take you to be with me that you also may be where I am.'
> *John 14:1–3*

I was younger, my children were still at primary school. A couple close to my husband and myself learned, at about twenty weeks into their pregnancy, that their third, much-wanted child suffered from a congenital heart condition. This meant he would survive only a few days after birth.

An immediate abortion was the proffered solution.

A difficult decision. After much deliberation they decided they wanted to allow their baby to grow to full term, with as natural a birth as possible. They were anxious to meet him, to love him, to know him, for his siblings to see him, and for him to die embraced by his family. Others might well make a different decision and I make no judgement; this was simply what my friends decided about their child.

My friend gave birth to J...... I arrived to see him at his home on the third day.

I remember my friend in bed with J...... in her arms, his father sitting on the bed with them. The baby had not been far from either of their arms since birth. As I looked at what seemed a perfect baby, his mother said his breathing had become laboured. As helpless onlookers, over the next minutes, we watched as his earth-life slipped away, his breathing becoming shallower and shallower.

We prayed together. Suspended in the presence of an extraordinary holy moment, his gentle last breath so peaceful. When someone's spirit passes from their body it remains a moment of great mystery.

Tears fell. A tiny baby who had only lived for three days. She asked if I would like to hold him. I held out my arms, embraced his still warm flesh and cuddled his now empty body.

He was beautiful.

There were no words. It was a time of supernatural peace. Grief and all its gut-wrenching and excruciating repercussions would come later. Deeply moved, I found the experience lived with me for weeks. It still does. Compelled to express the moment, I wrote this poem.

J......'s Coat

J...... we welcomed you,
we crowded round to meet you
we were so grateful to see you
touch you, hold you tight.
Never was a child more wanted
never was a child more blessed
never was there more evidence of God's hand
stretched out to

lovingly caress.
We caressed you too
enjoyed each and every moment
of your life touching ours.
of the reality of your living flesh.

We needed to know you.
To appreciate every tiny moment of your creation
knowing we would come face to face with fear.

Death, is this then your worst?
That a small bundle of loveliness
should move from life into eternity?

I thought it should have held more terror
than a peaceful moment of breath cut short;
that very beat of here and there
that very second, J...... transformed.
I saw his flesh part company
like a coat
gently sliding from his form
discarded, thrown away
an empty relic to an earthly life
that no longer held him fast.

His form fell still
silent, soft and empty,
an abandoned garment
still warmly pliable.
A movement from the loving cradle of his mother's arms
into the all-embracing tenderness,
the absolute security,

the total nourishment,
the pain free celebration,
of the actual living, breathing, tactile, eternal reality
of Jesus.[7]

I remain full of admiration for my friends. This tragedy did not cause them to lose each other and divorce. They continued to live well and eventually gave birth to a fourth child. As a couple they did not point a finger at God or blame Him but embraced Him as He embraced them. They faced death with open eyes and refused to run from reality. Their faith remained strong; they believed one day they would see their beloved son again.

Embracing mortality

To the small extent that we have any choice in this uncertain life, it is wise to face your own death. In a world where so many of our fellow human beings live with threats of terror and destruction, if you are lucky enough to imagine you might have any measure of control over how you die, that is a privilege that should not go to waste.

Euthansia?

Our deaths are the last message we leave for those we love. How my parents died — in comfort — was the way they cared for me after they were gone. I was not ready to lose them in my 20s, but they had prepared and so I was protected.

Their legacy to me was not a given.

---

[7] Ann Clifford, 'J......'s Coat', c.1992.

31

The illnesses that took them were outcomes that our past selves would have labelled catastrophic, worst-case scenarios. And yet for me these worst-case scenarios, though painful memories, are dwarfed by a much larger story: how my parents lived, how they died and how gracefully they did them both.

Alexandra Butler[8]

This quotation from Alexandra Butler is inspirational. Her call is for us to be brave and courageous in the midst of the uncertainty of life and exercise control over the only certainty. Her words help us to re-evaluate our dying and death not only in terms of ourselves, but also – and I suggest the more pressing consideration – in terms of those we will leave behind.

On occasion, for some of us, the experience of the dying and death of a loved one has been inspirational even if painful in the sense of loss. We were left with a sense of peace, of grace, and of a surprising beauty. A beauty that overshadowed the pain in the larger story of a person's life.

I have experienced one death where there were no barriers. There was honest, faith-filled communication, and full preparation outlined for the funeral/thanksgiving. The daughters had full knowledge of the will, the legacies and the estate. My much-loved friend, a daughter, reflected on how positive her opportunity to be with her

---

[8] Alexandra Butler, 'Experts on Aging, Dying as They Lived', http://opinionator.blogs.nytimes.com/. Search: Alexandra Butler. She is a poet and the author of *Walking the Night Road*, a memoir about losing her parents in her twenties.

mother was, on the increased depth of relationship once her mother entered the hospice. They often reflected on death. Her mother had a sense of expectation and wonder about meeting God. Death was a portal and, in talking together, they affirmed each other's faith.

When my friend Katrina now reflects back on that time, it is with a sense of gratitude. Her mother particularly delighted in the well-known story regarding the water bug that became a dragonfly, by Doris Stickney,[9] a story written ✳ to explain death to children, but equally lovely for adults.

The story explains that once the water bug had become a dragonfly he discovered a whole new life experience and longed to return and tell his friends, the water bugs, about his complete transformation. However, he realised, sadly, that he could never return to his old life under the water. His friends would simply have to wait for their own transformation to be able to understand.

But meeting death well isn't always the reality.

It is strange in our culture we find it so difficult to talk about the one thing that is a certainty for us all. Some deaths are more tragic than others because death arrives much sooner than expected. Lives hardly begun, like that of J … … Other lives are so beloved to us, so necessary for our lives to function, that we cannot face contemplating the possibility of their loss.

---

[9] Doris Stickney, *Water Bugs and Dragonflies: Explaining Death to Young Children (Looking Up)* (Cleveland, OH: The Pilgrim Press, 2004). I have it!

I wanted to include the Rev Canon Yvonne Richmond Tulloch's[10] story as a heart-rending illustration of what can happen if we don't prepare.

Sudden death

I was bereaved a few years ago when my husband Simon died, and from that I became acutely aware of the many problems people who lose a loved one can face – practically, emotionally, psychologically – even physically. And how bereavement can have a huge impact these days because there seems to be little understanding … & support is hard to find.

I was a minister of a Cathedral when Simon died and he had an international job. He died suddenly of a heart attack whilst away on business in Spain, and I received news of it one morning when I'd just arrived at work.

It was the kind of thing we all think will never happen to us.

My children were all away – 2 at uni – the eldest about to take her finals, and the middle one his first year exams – and our youngest was on a gap year in Uganda.

I was thrown into immediate shock and chaos.

I was faced with having to tell all the family – going to see his mother to tell her that her son had died, phoning *my* family.

Worse still the children – and get them home.

In fact I couldn't get hold of my youngest son, so we had to put an embargo on the news in case he

---

[10] Rev Canon Yvonne Richmond Tulloch, founder of www.Ata**Loss**.org.

found out on Facebook and boarded a flight that evening to Entebbe to bring him home.

Then I had to go to Barcelona to identify Simon's body and repatriate him. I discovered then that him dying as a foreigner in Spain meant I had few rights to make decisions or be informed. And I literally had to track down his (by then mutilated – through autopsy) body, and what I could of his possessions. Even his wedding ring was missing.

I had to do all of this in the midst of instant administrative chaos because Simon dealt with the paperwork in our house

– My car wasn't insured so I couldn't drive it initially.

– I couldn't change things to be able to use my phone.

– Worst of all were the bank accounts, most of which were instantly frozen, and I had no access to money.

Whilst this was going on there was the funeral to organise (where I was met with innocent questions like how much is your budget for this? And do you want to buy a grave for both of you?) And a big memorial service to organise at the Cathedral where the children and I bravely walked in, in front of some 800 people.

I assumed then that that was the worst of it over. But, even as a minister, who had been trained in these things, I knew nothing of how bad things would get.

The practical problems escalated:

– I spent the next 3 months trying desperately to deal with the administrative and financial chaos we were in. The paperwork and admin was overwhelming. I had to try to fathom where Simon had got to with things and where things were!

– There was uni to sort. My daughter was told she couldn't graduate because she had missed her finals, so she couldn't start her job,

– My son's return to uni to sort – he was told he would have to repeat the year because he hadn't taken *his* exams,

– My youngest son to get *into* Uni with no money to hand.

Probate was needed as quickly as possible, but that was difficult too as no one seemed to be able to tell me what I was entitled to. Meanwhile my financial problems were escalating.

So I had to get lodgers in to pay the bills, and then put the house on the market.

I was totally distressed; the bottom fell out of my life. I felt sick, I couldn't eat or sleep, I couldn't concentrate, remember things or function sufficiently enough even to do the most basic things of life, let alone the huge demands suddenly landed on me. I was lonely, I craved a hug, I feared the future and I didn't want to get up in the morning to face the day.

Everything crashed around me and it seemed like everywhere I turned, rather than being of help to me seemed to make matters even worse, and I didn't know where to turn for help.

If it wasn't for a friend taking me to the HTB The Bereavement Journey course – and another friend pointing out the Widowed Young ministry of Care For the Family, which I'd never heard of, I don't know what I'd have done.

Out of her experiences and recognition of the need for the bereaved to find help, Yvonne is the founder of www.Ata**Loss**.org, a website committed to ensuring that anyone in the UK who has suffered a significant loss can locate support. They continue to add to it.

Fear fills us at the thought of facing our own death.

> He too shared in their humanity so that by his death he might destroy him who holds the power of death – that is, the devil – and free those who all their lives were held in slavery by their fear of death.
> *Hebrews 2:14–15*

We have a choice.

We can ignore it, never prepare for it, and determine never to explore it. This strategy will not only make it difficult for us when dying beckons, it has the potential to make it excruciating for our families. Or we can look death in the eye, and prepare how we want to leave. We can empower ourselves and those we love, in the midst of utter disempowerment.

If we see death approaching because of a terminal illness, we can opt to tackle it with positivity. We might count ourselves fortunate to have time to prepare. Our story can become bigger than our dying.

But death arrives in unexpected ways. There is no guarantee we will have any time at all. There is much wisdom in making preparations.

As Christians we spend our lives learning to live not for ourselves but for Christ and for others. I wonder if in preparation for death we may continue to foster the same attitude.

We can die well so that those we love can continue with a sense of peace in their hearts and of thankfulness for our lives. As we go before them, we can be an example that affords a vision they could embrace – to live well and to leave well. As Alexandra Butler says, to do both gracefully.

Time to live

Dr Patrick Dixon,[11] who specialised in palliative care for the dying, explained during our conversation that he was always clear with his patients. When they had finished a round of chemotherapy, radiotherapy or any other therapy for the disease that was killing them, and were at their sickest, he would encourage them. He would explain that they would for a period grow in strength and wellness as they recovered from the treatment. Their enhanced health was a gift to be enjoyed however long it lasted. A gift to be revelled in, even if their condition was still terminal.

They were not yet dead, therefore now was the 'time to live'. He would ask: How would you like to embrace life right now?

---

[11] Dr Patrick Dixon: Futurist Keynote Speaker
www.globalchange.com.

Did they have a 'bucket list' (a number of experiences or achievements that a person longs for in their lifetime)? Were there things left undone? A dream they might still fulfil? He would encourage them to live a positive life in the 'now' time. This advice prompted me to make his words the title of this book.

> First I was dying to finish school and start more study.
> Then I was dying to finish study and start working.
> Next I was dying for my children to grow old enough for school, so I could return to work.
> Finally I was dying to retire.
> Now I am dying I suddenly realise I forgot to live.[12]

If we each could accept that we were dying, would we live a different life?

All fear is about fear of death. To live in fear of death is to miss life. Fear of death erases the present moment.

What might we change or engineer in the time we have left?

We find these questions difficult because most of us find self-reflection a challenging discipline. We prefer to fill ourselves with noise so we hear nothing.

Self-reflection is the most wonderful tool for listening, learning, changing and acting.

One of the greatest surprises to me was that God is ever-present to us. Ever ready to listen, to love, to speak and to empower. He is our place of refuelling in a busy, challenging life.

---

[12] Anonymous.

Do not underestimate Him.
Do not underestimate your ability to grow.
Dreams may still be honoured.

Do not be afraid …

The continuing journey

> Death is no more than passing from one room into
> another.
> But there's a difference for me, you know.
> Because in that other room I shall be able to see.
> *Helen Keller*[13]

We don't know what it means to die. We are all learners about dying. It is challenging to get our heads around. How to absorb the difficult and mind-numbing discovery we or someone we love has a terminal illness? Our natural reaction, when facing danger, is to fight or to fly.

Fighting is natural and important, and the medical services available to us are incredible. However, at some point intervention might no longer be relevant or desirable. We have a choice.

My lovely Sri Lankan friend Mary is now ninety. She is a widow and lives alone in her own home. She has a heart condition. The doctor offered her an operation to help her failing heart. After due consideration she decided against it. Not because of the real possibility she might die, an outcome she would not mind. Rather there is a real risk of

---

[13] Helen Keller, www.christianquotes.info Topics Death.

her having a stroke and then having to live with the medical repercussions.

Dr Atul Gawande in his remarkable book *Being Mortal*, which I recommend, makes one of many telling observations on his own profession.

> Our decision making in medicine has failed so spectacularly that we have reached the point of actively inflicting harm on patients rather than confronting the subject of mortality.[14]

Flight is an option, but we cannot outrun death. The more we run, the bigger the monster chasing us will grow in our imagination.

This book's journey is to explore a third way. To stand our ground, to open our eyes and face the monster. If we look, the tools to tackle it will be available.

Most of us resist this when we are healthy, able, alive, vibrant and young.

Gawande makes the point that understanding the finitude of one's life can be a gift:

> At least two kinds of courage are required in aging and sickness. The first is the courage to confront the reality of mortality – the courage to seek out the truth of what is to be feared and what is to be hoped … The second kind of courage – the courage to act on the truth we find. The problem is that the wise course is so frequently unclear… One has to decide

---

[14] Dr Atul Gawande, *Being Mortal* (London: Profile Books, 2015).

whether one's fears or one's hopes are what should matter most.[15]

An elegant single African woman in her early fifties I knew had self-medicated what she thought was severe back pain. As a consequence she had failed to seek professional medical attention for some time. Her eventual diagnosis was stage four pancreatic cancer. The doctors recommended medical intervention, and she endured several rounds of chemotherapy. Any statistic would tell you, with such a late diagnosis, the prognosis was bad. I am not sure she ever came to terms with the fact she would die.

Visitors arrived from her church. Workmates became regular visitors. She had worked for many years in the same company and a large amount of money was due after her death. She owned her flat. She was a strong, independent woman who held down a significant job.

Her death revealed to relatives she had not drawn up a will. She died an 'intestate' person. The ramifications were great regarding her estate.

The problem is, for us as Christians, we believe in healing, but it is evident and painful that God does not heal everyone. While we can pray for healing for our loved ones, for our friends and colleagues, to remain in a perpetual state of 'faith for healing' can make preparation for death difficult.

It can mean we don't have the conversations.

'Believing for healing' can act like a full stop. It can fail to allow the person to come to a place of peace with a sense

[15] Gawande, *Being Mortal*.

42

Esci ?

of God-anticipation, because they believe their illness persists because they 'lack the faith for healing'. They die a failure rather than looking forward to being embraced by the God who has loved them all their lives.

We fail to look at the whole picture. We don't allow ourselves to accept what is clear and inevitable. The whole church can be on its knees believing for healing and then the person dies. The ripples of hurt and anger rebound throughout the congregation, upending people's faith on what has now become an uncertain and storm-tossed sea. God is blamed. His ways are most certainly not our ways. Of course we must pray, but death is not the worst thing that can happen to us.

Death can strike us unexpectedly. I think of my friend Alan. I had known Alan for almost thirty years. Recently he and his wife found themselves once again living within five minutes of my husband and myself. I had been to his house with a few friends on the Tuesday night. We had eaten together. It was an enjoyable, easy evening. I was the last to leave.

Two day later, on Thursday night, Alan's wife left me two messages to ring her. I was at the theatre so my phone was off. When I returned home, I decided it was too late to call. I rang her about 8.30am the following day. She told me that Alan had died at work that Thursday afternoon. I had to ask her to repeat what she said because I couldn't grasp her words. I was profoundly shocked.

At work in his office, he stood up, crossed the room, told a joke, then fell and died. Of course, the paramedics came, an air ambulance arrived, but Alan was dead.

Sudden death

I jumped in the car and went to see her. I learned that a friend had picked up her call on the day of his death. He was the perfect person to be with her as she slowly tried to assimilate the agonising news.

My friend has dealt with, and continues to deal with, her loss with great dignity. Alan was a man of faith and she herself retains a deep life-enhancing faith. She remains living within their community of faith. She was not alone in her pain, and many were inspired by the hope-filled celebration of his life.

He was sixty-one years old and he had not prepared for his death. They had talked about it little. There was no will, and sorting everything out afterwards was a tremendous challenge.

His wife reflected her sadness at the swiftness of his death and their inability to say goodbye. My response was, 'He was a happy man.' Alan treasured his wife, his daughter and his life. One of his main delights was supporting his football team. My friend and he lived well together. Over the years they communicated the important things to each other. However, to be robbed of a last moment was excruciating and difficult. It was bewildering not to be sure of his partiality for a cremation or a burial. To have no knowledge of his preferences at his funeral was a painful experience. If a will had contained a personal message for either his wife or daughter should sudden death occur, it would have eased their sorrow. I recognise this is challenging, but what a salve and gift for your loved ones, left coping with unexpected tragedy.

The celebration of his life was magnificent. He loved God, and those who came were in no doubt of the richness

of his faith. His pride would have been immense at the
dignity his wife and daughter displayed as they shared his
life at the ceremony. He would have been delighted at how
his church family was tireless in their support of them.

Alan

Today it is difficult
to conjure a real person
of flesh and blood
suddenly gone
to inhabit somewhere beyond
yet near.
Near like the warmth of a fire
that spills onto the skin
far because,
like fire
touching him is not an option.

His life was skin close
Reaching, giving, holding, loving, caring.
He has gone to the light
where no shadows exist
only love inhabits
where time is no longer linear.

We are shaken –
Fallen like apples from the tree
Bruised and broken
By loss.

May brokenness yield many seeds
that will fall into the ground –

45

Joyce Dentist
East man Hosp.

burping
flatulence
loss of appetite
lost weight
2lbs in

Virtual
Colonoscopy
c Scan
Tumours in
peritoneum

polyp-
benign
remove as can
be cancerous

Colo-
Endos.

No pain
gas burping

Scan
Chest inf.
aggressive for
Ca
abd. Peritoneal
wall

6 weeks
ascites

Cancer under
stomach
like ovarian Ca
as no symptoms
Shoulder Tip
Pain   abdominal
referred pain from wind

A living dying that will harvest
life in all its fullness
For Another's glory.[16]

The cycle of grief

The fallout within the lives of family and friends when someone they love dies, is extensive. A truth bravely uncovered by Prince Harry, indicating his need for counselling twenty years after his mother's death. We should never dismiss death as something that is of little or no consequence. The effects of death are unalterable.

Death infuses living with value.

Elisabeth Kübler-Ross,[17] in her seminal book *On Death & Dying*, talks about the cycle of grief. It is likely to affect us all in some measure, in response to loss. Grief will touch us whether we are dealing with the prospect of our own death or the death of a loved one. Her findings are useful and constructive. Her words help us understand, name and adjust to the intense emotions that will beset us. A language for our complex journey helps us to understand ourselves and provides the words to communicate with others. Talking to the right person will lighten the load. We may not experience all the stages. They will not arise in any particular order. Each of us is unique. For myself, when experiencing intense grief, I was surprised it caused me to

---

[16] Ann Clifford, 'Alan', 2016.

[17] Elisabeth Kübler-Ross MD, *On Death & Dying* (New York: Scribner, 2014).

beat my chest with my fists. It was as if I needed somehow to physically attack the pain inside me. A completely unconscious reaction.

Denial

It is a seismic shock to receive news of the impending death of a loved one, or your own terminal illness. Perhaps we find it so difficult because, as Kübler-Ross suggests, our unconscious self believes, despite all evidence to the contrary, we will never die.

Numbness diffuses your body. Your brain goes into overload. Questions fill your mind, if not at the time, then afterwards. There must be a logical explanation. There is some mix-up or error. Different scenarios compete. Perhaps they have the wrong medical records? Is the doctor competent? You demand a second opinion, a third. You decide not to 'hear' in your being and continue to pursue life, rejecting any disturbing thoughts regarding dying or death. You buffer yourself against the news in any and every way. The word for this is 'denial'.

Death is less frightening to talk about when it is in the far distance rather than in our face. If we journey with someone as they attempt to come to terms with their own prognosis, it is important we interrogate our own attitude to death. We don't want our own fears and difficulties to overshadow another's journey. Our insecurities may push them into more testing, trying more doctors, casting around for any possible remedies, however bizarre. Our own inability to accept death may mean we will not allow them to accept theirs. It could inhibit our being an empathetic and genuine companion on their journey. Ascertaining the certainty of results is paramount. When the diagnosis is beyond question, continued denial can only become destructive.

Anger

Many of us are not good at expressing our anger, but often the questions accumulate. Why me? Why are others around me so healthy? Why should they inherit what I have worked so hard for? Why must I go through this? Why did I lose my best friend? Why, why, why? Envy, resentment and rage, feelings you never knew existed, can erupt.

It is important to give yourself permission to talk about these things. Acknowledgement of these feelings and expressing them is vital. Articulate them through writing, talking, raging with someone. Be creative.

The wise person recognises that expressing anger to everyone around will be hugely detrimental, not least to themselves. It will separate you from friends and family. Angry words can sound personal and the ones you love most might experience rejection and increasing alienation. You risk isolating yourself when what you need most is friendship and help.

A tool I suggest you pack for your journey as you read on is 'Attitude'. As long as you are expressing yourself to someone, then you can be free to cultivate an attitude of humility and generosity as you deal with the enormity of events before you.

Your friends and family will want to reassure you of your value and importance. Exercising wisdom and self-control over your emotions means you will not drive them away.

It is an interesting thought that neither our life nor our death is solely about self. How we live and how we face death, like our attitude, will create ever-extending ripples.

My mother-in-law died when she was eighty years old. She had married a popular vicar, who had been killed by a drunk driver after five years of marriage. Left a widow with two young children, she faced a life she had never expected. Trained as a primary school teacher, she returned to teaching for the next thirty years.

At her Celebration of Life service, I was astonished at the number who attended, including a significant group of her old pupils. She would have been heartened but bemused.

Don't underestimate how many lives your own will touch.

While you have life you have choice, and many more than you think will be watching.

Bargaining

There is a king in the Bible called Hezekiah[18] who became ill. The prophet Isaiah came to him and told him to put his house in order because his illness was terminal. Hezekiah, distraught with that prognosis, 'turned his face to the wall' and prayed to God. He reminded God that he was a

---

[18] See 2 Kings 20:1–11.

faithful follower. Before Isaiah reached home, God spoke again to His prophet. Isaiah returned to Hezekiah. He told the king God had heard his prayer and seen his tears. Hezekiah lived another fifteen years.

My friend prayed and asked God for fifteen more years. She died. She was fifty.

Whether you have faith in God or not, you may well want to bargain for further years. If you are 'good', if you make promises, perhaps God will grant your wish. Is there an agreement to be made with God to postpone the inevitable?

In your bargaining, deeper discomforts hidden away for some years can surface. Guilt, real or imagined, materialises. If you atone, the prognosis might change and additional years be granted.

Amazing things do happen for a few people. I believe in miracles, but I do not understand supernatural healing.

While rarely halting the inevitable, the urge to put things right is incredibly positive for its own sake.

Depression

Depression is predictable as you are hit by a huge sense of loss. The loss of the person you love so dearly. For those facing death, perhaps the loss of your body that functioned so well, incrementally degrading. Your life, with all your enjoyments, slipping away. The children/grandchildren you will never see born or grow. These are thoughts to ponder and talk through. It is a preparation for letting go, for gently releasing your dear ones and your world.

Perspective is a wonderful word; we let go to embrace something wonderful.

There are positive, constructive and life-affirming actions you can take in the midst of turmoil. Precious things can be given to a precious person. You will want a sense of continuity and remembrance of your real existence in time and space. This will help you to leave this world in peace.

Dr Micha Jazz,[19] a friend, musing on the prolonged death of his first wife of many years, Katie, reflected to me that he did not think we should be urged or expected to 'get over' loss. Without warning, he could, at times, be overcome with grief, for example while driving. Compelled to stop to recover, he would allow his sobs to run their course, then he would continue his journey. He had learned to let it happen.

While you might want to get through the raw, body-wracking, open wound sensation, the scar will not entirely disappear. Emotion can erupt and overcome you. It is normal. It doesn't mean that afterwards you cannot continue life, join with friends and enjoy their company, love life. There is a price you pay for daring to love another. Separation through death is deeply painful. The alternative is never to have known them as part of your life. An acceptable alternative? Of course not.

We all live with pain. We really do. We understand so little about each other. No wonder Jesus exhorts us to love,

---

[19] Dr Micha Jazz, writer, speaker and author of 'Be Still & Know' daily devotional in *Voice of Hope* (Premier Christian Radio).

forgive and live in harmony together, over and over and over again.

Acceptance

The final stage is one of acceptance; this is a gift that is not afforded to everyone. Sudden death is an agonising and difficult life experience. All the more reason to think these things through while we are able.

> We were neighbours for long, but I received more than I could give. Now the day has dawned and the lamp that lit my dark corner is out.
> A summons has come and I am ready for my journey.
> *Tagore*[20]

This is the place of accepting the inevitable; where you as a co-traveller on another's journey, or you as the terminally ill person, reach a place of rest and acceptance of approaching death.

There is much to accomplish on the journey, to reach a place of peace.

Work is needed to banish fear.

The rewards, as you labour to come to terms with death, mean that your final days on earth can be full of communion, companionship and hopeful expectation. It is a wonderful gift to leave behind.

---

[20] Kübler-Ross MD, *On Death & Dying*, p. 109, Rabindranath Tagore from Gitanjali, XCIII Nobel Prize-winning Bengali author.

Your reward, as you say goodbye, can be that nothing has been left unsaid, or undone, and grieving a life in its final moments can take place from a profound sense of hope-filled peace.

Resurrection hope

'I am the resurrection and the life. He who believes
in me will live, even though he dies.'
John 11:25

Jesus spoke these lines to Martha four days after her brother Lazarus died. She and her sister Mary struggled to understand why their beloved friend had failed to respond earlier to their request. They knew Jesus loved Lazarus. Why hadn't He prevented the death of their brother? They understood their brother's healing was not dependent upon 'the healer' being present. It seemed their friend had abandoned them at the moment of their greatest need.

In his final miracle before his crucifixion on the cross and His own death, Jesus confronted what was not only going to happen to Him, but also to every single human being who lived on earth – death. He wept for the death of His friend. He wept for the pain that death caused.

In this miracle Jesus defined His divinity and what He had come to do. In a few words He commanded life back into a dead man who then walked from his grave with his grave clothes loosening around him.

It must have been astonishing. Not only for the spectators, but for Lazarus himself. What a story he had to tell!

Through His own death on the cross and later resurrection, verified by numerous witnesses, Jesus made good on His promise of life to everyone who believed in Him.

A promise true until the end of this space–time continuum.

> Death is the prerequisite to resurrection, the new life God intends.
> *John Ortberg*[21]

In Revelation 21, John wrote that, because of the resurrection of Jesus, death was now no longer the end of the story. Tears and pain would, at the end of time, pass away. God's long-term plan embodied full restoration. His intention – to make His home with men and women, in a new heaven and a new earth.

That includes you and me.

---

[21] John Ortberg, *Who Is This Man?* (Grand Rapids, MI: Zondervan, 2012).

Chapter 2
Facing Our Fears

Only when we are no longer afraid do we begin to live
Dorothy Thompson[22]

The images of death in our head are often media-induced as most of us have never seen a dead body, though we might have attended a funeral. In the UK it is unusual to have an open casket where the dead are visible. While there is time for the family to view the dead at the undertakers', our latter historical custom is a closed coffin. Funerals customarily include professional solemn men and women dressed in black who attend to the coffin. They stand, silent sentinels, heads bowed, respectful and mournful.

Things are changing. Many prefer a Celebration of Life service/memorial to which friends and colleagues are invited. The burial or cremation is a quiet family affair a day or two before or immediately prior to the public memorial.

It is rare that media images regarding death are positive or life-affirming. Often in film, death is portrayed to induce in us the dramatic, spine-tingling fear experience.

---

[22] Dorothy Thompson, American journalist and radio broadcaster, www.goodreads.com.

It is unsurprising thoughts regarding genuine death become a practice we will shy away from. I suspect, as we grow older, fewer of us watch those fear-inducing movies.

No doubt you will laugh, but I remember *Jaws* playing in cinemas in 1975. I read the publicity and decided not to watch the film. Why? I love swimming in the sea. If I watched it, with my sensibilities, it would terrify me and erode my enjoyment of the open water. Not true for everybody! I had dealt with fear in my life, I didn't need to invite it to return.

If we face our fears, then we will need time to collect our thoughts and reflect – a challenging prospect because when we stop, the noise that fills our lives throws toddler tantrums and emits loud cries for attention. I have a reflection book. I scribe the clamour inside which helps me ignore it. It clears my head for fresh thought.

> Reflection is like eating a piece of fruit. Sometimes we eat fruit because we like it, and want it, sometimes because we know it's good for us.

Reflection feeds my soul. I may read an informative book, scripture, write out quotations, thoughts, worries, prayers, dreams – above all, I stop and meditate.

Documenting your journey is a wonderful and positive way to release your feelings and gain unexpected insight.

Suggestions:

- A lovely book to write your thoughts. Why not use a fountain pen?

- A sketchbook to draw pictures to express yourself – purchase a pack of fabulous coloured pencils.

- Create a new file JOURNAL on your tablet, laptop or desktop computer.

- Use your phone to take pictures to illustrate the journey.

- Create a scrapbook and collect pictures, poems, words, Bible passages, quotations.

- Explore Pinterest.

- Record your thoughts and stories on your phone or camera.

When we look back at what we discovered, our present can be reinvigorated and strengthened.

The process of dying

Dying concentrates the mind wonderfully well on what
we truly believe
and unveils what we do not.

Many major events we face in life are scary. Preparation is everything. Some need more groundwork than others.

We've all faced exams. My most stressful was my driving test. When the examiner declared I had passed, I burst into tears. I was seventeen years old.

We arrange what we need for that celebratory party, an eighteenth, a twenty-first, a fiftieth.

We do our research before a job interview.

The decision to get married is huge. It demands thought, consultation and communication. There is a deluge of preparation for your one special day. Do you choose a registry office or a religious service, or both? Together a couple will carefully evaluate the form of their public declaration. The post-wedding celebration with family and friends, for most, will require months of organisation.

Preparation to have a child can take years. Some will need medical intervention, IVF treatment; others will adopt. Whatever route is taken, this will take months, even years, of planning. Longing translates into delight when we embrace our child in our arms. Many then desire a public acknowledgement of such a gift, arranging a christening, a naming, or a ceremony of welcome into the church family. A party is likely to follow.

I remember visiting my father in Holland, where he lived with his second wife. We visited a local park where stood a large steel pole with a viewing platform wrapped around it, similar to the construction built in Brighton, although not as high. I was excited as I love a bird's-eye view: I can orientate myself, as I am geographically challenged. I'm the one who finds getting out of paper bags difficult!

As it ascended, I stood at the edge of the platform enjoying the vertical drop as the ground receded from us. I turned to express my delight to my dad, to find him standing as if surgically attached to the wall in the centre of the lift. He could see nothing. I glanced at his face with a sudden recognition of his terror. I encouraged him to take a step and stand nearer the window. He responded with an emphatic 'No'.

We have a choice with dying. We can orientate ourselves by looking firmly at what is unfolding in front of us, and gain perspective. We may gain a sense of time. We can certainly bring order. We can also choose our ideal where and how. The alternative is to live in a fog, hope for the best, and if and when anything occurs, ache for it to be quick and painless.

My father died in Holland in his own house, his wife having died seven months earlier that same year. My two sisters and I, his sole carers, watched over him during the last week of his life. I had visited a few months earlier, after his diagnosis of cancer of the spine. I recognised he would not recover from this and wanted to discover his preferences regarding his funeral. It was difficult. He was of a different generation. He had fought in the war as an eighteen-year-old. He didn't want to talk. He didn't want to die. We didn't have a clue how to help him.

In Holland a person must be buried or cremated within seven days. We were shocked when the funeral director arrived to interview us seven hours after his death. He inundated us with never-ending questions. The one and only comfort, apart from the three of us bonding together, was that we had some idea of what he wanted.

The process of dying appears too scary, we don't want to look. We don't want to prepare.

A ComRes[23] survey found the following:

---

[23] ComRes interviewed 2,085 British adults online between 15th and 17th April 2016. Data were weighted to be representative of British adults aged eighteen plus. Data can be found at www.comresglobal.com. Search: Dying Matters Coalition – Public Opinion on Death and Dying.

- 30% of British adults say they feel uncomfortable discussing dying with family and friends.

- 35% say they have written a will.

- 33% say they have registered to become an organ donor or have a card.

- 25% say they have talked to someone about their own end-of-life wishes.

- 7% say they have written down any of their wishes or preferences about their future care should they become unable to make decisions themselves (15% in 65+ group).

- 1% say they have initiated a conversation with their GP about their end-of-life wishes.

- 30% say they have done none of these (only 9% in 65+ group).

These figures show the majority of us are completely unprepared. Why don't we plan for it?

In formulating our desires, we can moderate our fear. We can care for our family. Many recount that, although they were initially hesitant, once decisions were finalised it enabled them to 'rest easy'. It brought a sense of comfort. Under 'Practicalities' in the second half of this book I outline ways to help us think through our preparation.

We could change our perspective. My father stood away from the view, too scared to look. If we see the whole of life as a preparation for death, perhaps what is truly important will snap into focus.

Jesus replied: '"Love the Lord your God with all your heart and with all your soul and with all your mind." This is the first and greatest commandment. And the second is like it: "Love your neighbour as yourself." All the Law and the Prophets hang on these two commandments.'
Matthew 22:37–40

Love God; love others; love yourself. The biblical teaching brings what is eternal to earth and unpacks a practical way to live. We are spiritual beings made to be in relationship with God. Recognising His perfect love for us will help us face our fear and overcome it. Reminding ourselves of the need to continue to love ourselves and those around us will only enhance the time we have left.

Fear of suffering

In our unconscious we cannot perceive our own death and do believe in our own immortality.
Elisabeth Kübler-Ross[24]

What I worry about is what is going to happen on the road to death.
A patient
Elisabeth Kübler-Ross[25]

I confess that even if I can come to terms as much as possible with the idea I will actually die, I don't want to suffer. Historically, suffering and pain were an integral

---

[24] Kübler-Ross MD, *On Death & Dying.*
[25] Kübler-Ross MD, *On Death & Dying.*

part of life, today we have access to more pain relief than ever. Hospice and palliative care (now termed supportive care) offer tremendous assistance. The National Council for Palliative Care (NCPC, www.ncpc.org.uk) is an umbrella charity for all those involved in palliative, end-of-life and hospice care in England.

Living and maintaining a health-filled lifestyle of exercise, balanced eating, positive mental and emotional states and enrichment of our souls, are solid choices to make for our general well-being. Wise choices to continue as long as possible even with a terminal diagnosis.

I discovered life insurance companies bemoan the fact we don't construct financial provision for living the length of years the longevity tables now predict. We tend to underestimate the length of our lives. I don't remember who said this in a conversation one day years ago, but I took note.

> If I had realised I would live so long, I would have taken better care of myself.[26]

There is much we can do to determine how we wish our lives to end. For example: How much medical intervention? Who can make decisions on our behalf if we cannot? This I cover in Practicalities, under 'Lasting Power of Attorney' and 'Advance Decision (Living Will)'.

It is important to recognise that it is not automatic that next of kin will be the decision-makers. I was shocked when I discovered this. Without documentation, the medical profession will decide your medical care. Ask the

---

[26] Anonymous.

question: would I like to be kept alive at all costs? Thinking these things through for ourselves will prepare us and bring comfort to our loved ones.

We cannot choose how we will die, but we can choose to trust God with our life and our death. A life of faith is putting one foot in front of the other with our eyes fixed on Him. It is not about the preservation of our body, but our spirit/personality/essence becoming more like the One whom we long to meet face to face.

Fear of loss of control

We need not be a control freak to worry about losing any or all ability to look after ourselves. Most of us are fiercely independent, but things will change. Our bodies are designed to deteriorate. Yet whatever physical loss of control might be in store for us, or has already occurred in our lives, our spirit may remain invigorated, alert, vibrant and continue to develop until its release in death.

Life is uncertain. We do not know the future, but God does not want us to live in fear. There are things we can control and things we cannot. The trick is to grasp what we can achieve and relinquish what we cannot.

We can take a fresh survey of our relationships. Maybe with age our priorities might adjust. Time is a precious gift that allows the unveiling of perspective.

We can give attention to our physical, mental and emotional wellness. None of us want or need to live with anxiety and stress. Perhaps for the first time in our lives we might experiment with techniques to relax and de-stress.

I recognise the methods we might choose to achieve this will vary according to our beliefs; however, there are innumerable choices: a contemplative space, a retreat centre, or the simplicity of purchasing a machine for a regular foot massage.

We can enhance our spiritual lives through reading, studying and prayer. More contemplation, less action, but greater purpose, perspective and, perhaps, influence.

We live by faith in working on what is within our control, as well as what is not.

Attitude

> Attitude is like a stone dropped in water
> Its ripples extend over a whole lake.

Much we cannot change in our lives, but one thing remains ours and ours alone – our attitude.

Journeying with someone as their life on earth ends is demanding. How can you be the best for them and for yourself? Your attitude can help or hinder.

Living with pain, constant hospitalisation and drugs is a tortuous journey. What will be your attitude in the whole process? As the one who is facing death, you might believe you have rights.

Our will determines our attitude. Whatever your position in the current state of affairs, how might you aspire to greet each new day?

We can make it so difficult for people to look after us. A sense of entitlement to indulge in a grumpy, irritable and unpleasant attitude, as you are the one dying, will isolate you.

A martyr who incessantly complains about the care they are dispensing will make it unbearable for the one they care for.

Friends and family will grow reluctant to visit or involve themselves if we cultivate a self-absorbed, critical and bad-tempered demeanour.

However, do not be tempted to live a lie. A false godliness by protestations – I am fine; I am coping well with life – when deep inside you are broken and lost, is disastrous. A life-giving attitude is not about profound and unhealthy denial. We must be real and allow ourselves to be damaged, vulnerable, fearful, hurting people. We are deeply human. Loved ones and carers will want to support the bad days and be there to enjoy the good days, if we exercise self-control.

A woman – let's call her Diane – had a profound Christ-centred spiritual experience. Diagnosed a short time afterwards with a terminal illness, the disease took its course and she finally lapsed into unconsciousness. She remained comatose for a long time, which upset her daughter, also a God-lover. She could not understand why her mother remained alive. It was baffling and upsetting.

Diane's friends continued to visit her, to sit with and talk to her despite her persistent unresponsiveness. One by one the friends, who followed a different religion, recognised the palpable spiritual change in their unconscious friend.

When Diane died, the funeral was packed. During the service her friends heard of Diane's moving and impactful spiritual experience which had enriched and enlightened the last months of her life.

As the friends talked together after the funeral, they recognised Diane's profound influence on each of them. It was a deep comfort to her daughter when the friends shared their experience. She concluded that, despite her mother being devoid of all function, God had waited to conclude His purposes in her.

> The strongest people are not those who show strength in front of us, but those who win battles we know nothing about.[27]

Fear of loss of loved one(s)

When diagnosed with a life-shortening illness, you may find thinking and talking about it traumatising. You and your loved ones understand the prognosis is poor, but find speaking about the 'elephant in the room' too difficult. You don't want to 'upset' each other, despite the reality that everyone is distressed anyway.

Perhaps you are elderly. You recognise more years lie behind you than ahead of you, yet fear keeps you silent. Fear raises its head whenever someone you love dies, or you have a health scare. Death could strike you, but you stay silent.

The courage to look, learn, share and uncover your real frame of mind concerning what is happening to you, should not find you stripped bare and unable to cope. Why not grasp the opportunity to empower yourself? Openness

---

[27] Anonymous.

and transparency can yield a most comforting freedom. Sharing our lives with the right person is relational, bonding and life-enhancing. If you connect with one person, those new words to share with others you love, and who love you, will become a precious, freshly discovered vocabulary.

To be transparent and vulnerable may feel scary, as if we are revealing the gnarled, ugly and unsightly parts of ourselves. Hosting such lies about ourselves keeps us silent. Truth-talking with the right people has the power to transform all things into unique and positive milestones.

We in Britain are famous for our stiff upper lips. I grew up not expressing my reality. Children were 'seen and not heard'. This upbringing helped me understand, when I had my own children, how crucial it was to talk of emotions in order that they might gain expressive words for their reactions.

Throughout my childhood and teenage years there was a dam inside me. The wall had to grow ever higher because the pent-up emotion within me found no expression. The possibility of it bursting was terrifying.

When I recognised I needed and wanted help, I asked and was fortunate enough to receive it. I remain extremely grateful for the time and effort of different people. I still find it difficult to express what is going on inside. My make-up is such that I absorb things, and I need time to recognise their impact. What happens is that emotion builds up and implodes within me and inside I am in pieces. What I need is a revelation regarding the thoughts revolving in my head. A perspective on any unhelpful reactions I have expressed and need to apologise for. I know I need to talk, and when clarity comes, I find a wise friend as soon as possible.

So many of us are frightened of emotion, and instead of allowing either ourselves or others to express themselves, we do everything to keep the lid on. Why? Difficult times in life elicit difficult emotions. We all need a safe place to speak and discover words for the intensity of our circumstances. It can be enormously refreshing and healing to do so.

Fear of telling children

This fear of emotion extends to how we treat our children. We fear their reaction if we tell them the truth. In my experience, giving a child a clear, age-appropriate explanation of the present circumstances, and what the immediate future looks like, is extremely helpful to them. They are resilient, and the danger is that, if you do not allow them to join your journey, they will journey isolated and alone.

A child understands if something bad is happening. If we don't involve them they have a habit of blaming themselves. If we include them, they will learn an enormous number of life skills. Children's contributions to the dying person, and those grieving, can be huge. Silence at such a time is failing to give them value as human beings.

Terrible things do happen to many youngsters and families. The oppression of silence, secrecy, and the inability to speak what is true, damages the most. Injury can resonate like a bell throughout entire lives.

I talked to a friend with several children, who lives within a large Christian community. She reflected that her children recognise they are part of a life cycle of conception – birth – life – death – resurrection; these states continue in an unbroken link.

In her own family's life, she gave birth prematurely to a perfect baby just before twenty weeks. Doctors told them premature birth was a possibility, and for days they had prayed for the life of their daughter. It was not to be. It was a difficult and heart-breaking time to hold their tiny dead baby in their arms. They named her. They knew they must tell their other two children of their sibling. Both my friend and her husband chose to make themselves vulnerable with them. If they explained, they could, as a family, grieve together.

The children knew their mum and dad were in pain; explanation brought a new depth to their relationships. As they dealt with the pain together, they could recognise their parents' faith, despite their grief. The death of the child did not mean that God was untrustworthy.

We don't have many answers, but for them it meant that one of their immediate family had gone ahead of them into the presence of Jesus.

This community has their own graveyard. They lay out the dead person themselves. They sit with the body and remember the importance of that person in their life.

It is sobering and final seeing the body of a real person, part of your community, laid out prior to burial. Someone you had perhaps spoken to the day before, who now lies dead. It is not a place of fear. This is not a media death. It is a place for reflection and farewell. To say goodbye, together.

My friend believes there is something heaven-bound about a person near death which a small child recognises with more ease and peace than an adult. It sits well with them, and the most boisterous child will sit quiet and still, rightly respectful.

The Bible talks about becoming like a child[28] in order to understand the things of God. As adults, our fears often cause us to run away. We do not want our children to catch our fear. Perhaps we should be open to catching their simple acceptance.

Rio Ferdinand, in the moving BBC One documentary *Being Mum and Dad*[29] had three children to bring up after his wife died from cancer at the age of thirty-four in 2015. It was his love for his children that drove him to seek help for them. One of the beautiful things he learned through meeting different people with the same experience was the idea of a Memory Jar. The children and he took time to write memories of Rebecca, their mum, and put the notes in the jar. His young daughter was so delighted she resolved to write something every day. Any time they wished to remember they could rifle the jar and read some memories. Initially sceptical of therapy for himself, his love for his children took him on a journey. Their journey opened him up to his own pain. He says he started to feel he could breathe a little. He could allow himself to remember specific moments with her. The notion of

---

[28] Matthew 18:3–4.

[29] Rio Ferdinand, *Being Mum and Dad*, BBC One, shown 12th April 2017.

therapy for himself was something he had now become comfortable to pursue. Children have much to teach us.

Fear of isolation and not being heard

Only humility can negotiate the bridge to understanding.

Sharing what you feel, what you think and what you want needs time and space. With illness, age or inexperience, formulating and communicating your thoughts can challenge the special people in your lives. Your family may not be comfortable talking as candidly as you. Vulnerability is a choice both you and your loved ones need to make. You might consider finding a bridge. People bridges come in many shapes and sizes, from different walks of life. The function of a 'person-shaped' bridge is to help two people who stand on opposite banks of a river, to meet. Each must choose whether to walk across and connect.

Communicating with authority in any form, be it medical, social or financial, can be tough. You can find yourself passive, silent and frustrated as you submit to decisions made regarding you and your care. The alternative is to use your bridge person, a patient listener who will help you to discover the words you need. You may prefer a book into which you write what you want to say, having pondered your choices. At the right moment you can then read aloud what you want to express. You need to say what works for you. An informed question means access to all the information and expertise available. Keep asking until you are satisfied.

This is where creative thinking, while healthy and full of well-being, can allow you to outline your wishes in advance. (See 'Practicalities'.) This will mean choices made are treated with respect and consideration. This will also inform any future choices you make as your healthcare unfolds. A practical readiness means that, as your symptoms and the prognosis deteriorate, you will be well prepared to understand and accept with fortitude and faith what lies ahead. Choices will coalesce and simplify. Meaningful dialogue can now occur which will dismantle any isolation. The knowledge that you are heard and understood releases pent-up stress.

As you face your fears with others alongside you, you can live life from a place of calm. Take time to talk with one or two regarding your fears: of the loss of loved ones; of being unaccompanied on your journey; your apprehension and fear of the unknown; ease will come. The very act of sharing and praying should bring comfort and peace.

The alternative is separation. Imagine you are a castle. Outsiders become enemies to defend yourself against. A swift tug and the drawbridge to your life slams shut. A no-entry sign is posted. Living your life in a state of terror of death is tortuous. I entreat you not to live your life in this way.

There is a joyous and enriching way to live available to every one of us, despite terrible agonising struggles. Joy is a gift to be found in unexpected places in delightful ways.

We all need a friend or two who will share our space.

Speak in such a way that others love to listen to you. Listen in such a way that others love to speak to you.[30]

Why is it that many of us reason we should journey alone? Do we believe we should solve life's puzzles by ourselves?

Our childhood does and can be relentless in defining our adulthood. Maybe we have struggled in our relationships. Perhaps deep relationships are scary. We shy away from intimacy, afraid to make ourselves vulnerable.

I call myself a life-learner. Growing up was a complex time for me, with parents in a deteriorating marriage, who finally divorced when I was twelve. I existed with a fog of misunderstanding in my head, because children were not communicated with in a truthful way. I did not understand why life changed so catastrophically around me. I found intimacy a huge challenge. Trusting others seemed unnatural.

Perhaps nobody springs to mind with whom you could talk. A person of faith, a vicar, a priest can be helpful, even if you are uncertain regarding faith yourself. Most are willing to listen to doubts, concerns and fears. There is an Association of Christian Counsellors (http://www.acc-uk.org). There are counselling directories for different regions, sites to help you find the specific therapist you require. A therapist can be a positive solution if you cannot speak to anyone you know, including family. Your doctor may well be able to help you find a counsellor.

---

[30] Anonymous.

Community became important to me. I live within a caring network from whom I have learned a great deal. I have, during difficult times, needed and sought professional assistance.

I am grateful to those who heard my cries for help and came alongside me. Do be brave and discover the freedom of learning to share intimately with another person.

> Owning our story and loving ourselves through the process is the bravest thing we will ever do.
> *Dr Brené Brown*[31]

Allow yourself to be loved

Whom do you love, who loves you? As you share what is happening, you may be surprised by the people who come alongside you. Welcome those that approach you positively, happy to dialogue. Try not to judge those that find it too difficult.

I regret not giving enough support to a good friend when the illness she battled received the diagnosis of stomach cancer. At the time, several members of my family were dying, including my father. Another close friend died of a catastrophic heart attack, leaving a widow and children. I struggled to cope. I wish I had been stronger for her sake and mine.

Challenging news is an opportunity for family rifts and difficulties to pale into insignificance. We will look at this in more depth later.

---

[31] Brené Brown, 'The Hustle for Worthiness',
www.ordinarycourage.com.

Meaning-making

As human beings, one of our deepest needs is to make meaning of our lives. This need impels us to 'make our mark'. Victor Frankl's helpful thinking encourages us that just because death approaches it does not mean that life ceases to expect something from us. Or indeed God Himself, if we love Him. While impending illness may appear to curtail our lives, slowly miniaturising them, there is still much we can contribute to others that is life-enhancing and important.

We are part of existence far greater than ourselves alone. Careful analysis will give us the chance for meaningful decisions.

Fear that life has been meaningless – or has it?

> How many regrets, how many battles, how many
> mistakes?
> Yet this is not my sum.
> Today I live.

Power rests in me, to give, to love, today.

Research suggests most people's number one fear is living a meaningless life.[32] We are surrounded by images of people who achieved amazing things. Their contribution to humanity is enormous. Compared to the

---

[32] Richard J. Leider and David A. Shapiro, *Repacking Your Bags: Lighten Your Load for the Good Life* (San Francisco, CA: Berrett-Koehler Publishers, 2012).

number of people in the world, few of us have an impact beyond our immediate lives. It does not mean we are failures. What does a meaningful life look like? I chart it by the depth and quality of relationships we enjoy. Notice I did not say by the 'number'. An ever-growing quantity of social media followers does not a meaningful life make. A meaningful life is about learning to love and allowing ourselves to be loved.

We find it difficult to own that we are intrinsically valuable, each as a unique human being. The less self-worth we have the more anxious we are likely to be. Why do we spend so much energy hiding our lack of it?

We work hard to buffer our self-esteem. By education; the job we worked so hard to succeed in; the amount of money we earn; the things we can afford; the youth-enhancing procedures or anti-aging steps we take; our exercise-driven body and many more. Or we decide we are failures and our self-respect hits rock-bottom.

As we face our own death and reflect on what is significant in our lives, it will be our relationships. Our relationships will be many and varied. We are somebody's child. There are siblings, schoolmates, workmates, further education mates, husband, wife, children, etc. Who is special? It is the breakdown of these relationships, with damaged bonds, eroded trust, connections severed for many years, that haunts us. This is what causes a pain that medication cannot touch.

We are of immense value in a significant world. Known and loved by God before we were formed in the womb, we are irreplaceable human beings.

As we learn to accept ourselves for who we are, neither as a failure nor as an achiever, this will buffer us against anxiety.

Perhaps there are situations, on reflection, we regret, and we are sorry. We might want to put stuff right; historic events in our lives, where we need to ask for forgiveness, suddenly come into focus. Write down your thoughts and determine to do something about what you write.

We are not yet dead, there remains time to live. Time to bring healing and hope into the desolate places we have played a part in creating. Time to continue to learn to love others. Love costs. It cost Jesus everything.

C. S. Lewis describes heart-rendingly the cost of loving in his book *The Four Loves*. He explains that love makes us vulnerable to the point of our hearts being torn apart. We may have goods, property, work, all of which will anaesthetise us from the possibility of pain. Scarily, we will find we have abandoned ourselves to isolation, and our capacity for love will decrease.

> Love means learning to give ourselves away completely.
> Without love life remains a mystery.

At the worst points in my life, when I was hopeless and helpless, I concluded that, however difficult life became, there were three things I could do:

- I could choose to love God.

- I could choose to love my family.

- I could choose to love others.

These choices have continually brought me through the black times and, without me realising, sowed seeds into my future, helping me to love myself and others. Now older, reflecting on what I may have achieved is not what excites me. What truly makes my heart sing are my relationships:

Not everyone has this ✓

- One of my adult children ringing me, excited with news to share.
- Another messaging me to ask whether they can stay.
- A friend who wants to buy me a present.
- A new life born into the family.
- A wander in an art exhibition with an old friend.
- Supporting a friend at a funeral.
- My husband inviting me on a date.

Countless moments of joy, pain, tears and excitement.

I continue to learn how to love others and it remains one of the greatest joys of my life.

> Not all of us can do great things,
> but we can do small things with great love.
> *Mother Teresa*[33]

My greatest love relationship, that underpins every other, is the one I pursue with God.

---

[33] Mother Teresa, quoted on www.goodreads.com.

I remember, as a relatively new Christian, recogi
was isolated and alone. Deep relationships were a my
One day, from a television programme playing ii
background where I lived, some words rang out like a bell
in my head. *'It's easier to love the whole world than it is to love
one person.'* Those words were a profound challenge. I
realised that loving God in isolation would not be enough.
A deep spiritual life was not my only goal. Learning to love
another human being, a person with skin on their face,
became a task I should also accept. My poor husband was
the one tasked with that!

Fear of the unknown

As we ponder on death, it is inevitable our thoughts will
reach out to some spiritual being, a Creator, to God, His
existence and the meaning of life. Fears and worries locked
inside us for years can surface and cause a great amount of
upset and anxiety.

Finding faith in a God who tenderly cradles us in our
freefall from life can bring peace to the turmoil in which we
find ourselves.

Many of us worry about the notion of heaven and hell
and where we might find ourselves after death. The God
of the Bible, made known as a human being through Jesus,
is a spectacularly generous God. Whether we have known
Him for years or ask Him to come to us as we die, He will
receive us and enfold us. Why wait? I encourage you to
explore the spiritual. You have nothing to lose by doing so,
and everything to gain.

Kayla Mueller was a twenty-six-year-old aid worker held captive for months by ISIS. She wrote this to her family.

> I remember mom always telling me that all in all in the end the only one you really have is God. I have come to a place in experience where, in every sense of the word, I have surrendered myself to our creator b/c literally there was no else … and by God and by your prayers I have felt tenderly cradled in freefall.[34]

She never returned home. She was killed in April 2015.

But that is not the end of her story, and it will not be the end of mine.

Fear of losing hope

Hope sees the invisible, feels the intangible
And achieves the impossible
Helen Keller[35]

As I reflected on hope, I eyed the small area I had sown with thyme rather than grass seed. I trim it regularly, but in the summer I allow it to grow and flower. Why? Because then the bees come. The whole bed becomes alive to the sight and sound of bees focused on pollination and nectar collection, the sweet liquid in the colourful, tiny, pink/purple flowers, to produce honey. I am honoured that

---

[34] Kayla Mueller letter, www.theguardian.com/us-news/2015.
[35] Helen Keller, www.quotbook.com.

they found my west London garden. I love that they visit us with their inspiring presence and I relish watching their diligence.

Bees find nectar in many and diverse places. They hunt for it. They work hard to collect and transport it back to their hive. In Greek mythology, nectar was the drink of the gods. It had magical properties to confer immortality on anyone who had the 'luck' to drink it.

Nectar is available for each of us. It resides in the person of Christ. A human being who died yet did not stay dead. A resurrected man, alive still and offering life to us. He embodies hope.

> In his great mercy [God] has given us new birth into a living hope through the resurrection of Jesus Christ from the dead, and into an inheritance that can never perish, spoil or fade … kept in heaven for you.
> *1 Peter 1:3–4*

Chapter 3
Our Future

Fear of death is a natural fear. Whether we live with fear is a choice. God does not want us to live fearful lives. His peace, His grace and His kindness are available. The key question is – do you trust Him?

My experience in learning to trust God comprises a multitude of decisions, and a lifetime of learning. Each difficult decision or agonising circumstance requires placing myself before Him once again to ask for His help. When I lie dying, I will ask once again. I will need help to trust Him to bring me into His comforting, all-encompassing, love-filled presence.

As you breathe your last breath, your essence, your personality, your spirit, will move from the physical time–space world you previously inhabited into an alternative habitation, filled with the presence of Jesus, the Spirit and the Father.

Paul, so captivated by the notion of being with Jesus, finds himself conflicted. He desires to die and be with Christ,[36] but recognises much remains to do. You too have a rich contribution, whatever your prognosis. As His beloved child, God has purpose for you.

---

[36] Philippians 1:21–24.

When Jesus returns in triumph we shall be resurrected, along with all who have died loving God. We shall receive our new bodies, which will be eternal. They will not decay, run down, run out or die. They will be immortal, and together we will rule and reign with Him in the newly created heaven and new earth. Love will rule and there will be no tears, no fear, no death, but only living with Him in a wholly incorruptible new way of life, a unique joyous reality. We will become the community of faith God always intended.[37]

New bodies

If we read the Gospel accounts of the resurrected Jesus meeting with all manner of persons, they indicate what a resurrected body incorporates. He can walk and talk with people, as on the road to Emmaus, and yet be unrecognised. He can prepare and eat food. He can travel through walls. Jesus remains Himself, yet bafflingly different.

Judgement

There will be judgement. It is inescapable.

Grace is a free gift from God given to all who believe in Him. When we are our best selves we might exhibit unselfish love, kindness, compassion, generosity both of spirit and of means. Nothing we do could match the goodness and purity of God. Therefore, we cannot escape

---

[37] Tom Wright, *Surprised by Hope* (London: SPCK, 2012).

His final judgement on a world where, at its worst, horror piles upon horror, and which, at its best, is never free from self-interest. We are full of complexities built on selfishness.

From the beginning God committed Himself to the salvation of His creation. He became a human being through Jesus. This sinless God–man showed us the personhood of God. He showed His total commitment to our complete well-being by dying an unjust and terrifying death. This resurrected God–man waits alongside God the Father to welcome and deliver every single person who believes in Him from judgement. Without Jesus, that judgement separates us from immortality in God's new heaven and new earth.

None of us can earn or work our way to a purity that allows us to stand before a pure and good God. We can only stand in the purity of Jesus who has given His life for us.

I will face judgement. God is a God of justice and He will judge me beyond my earth life into eternal life. God will not be mocked. What has been done (spoken)[38] in secret will be shouted from the rooftops. God will reveal Himself to embody justice and fairness. My judgement will be public yet determined by another human being – Jesus, the God–man who understands every nuance of humanity. God's review of my life is scary as I know the frailties of my heart and the things I have done. However, I trust Him. He loves me so much that Jesus died for me.

---

[38] See Luke 12:3.

Therefore, there is now no condemnation to those who are in Christ Jesus.
Romans 8:1

God will judge His creation against His purity. There is much wickedness in this world. Men and women continue to do unconscionable deeds to each other. Children are abused in abominable ways. Whole people groups are annihilated. War always continues somewhere in our world. Money and power are but two of many idols served by innumerable people at the expense of hundreds and thousands. God sees all and forgets nothing unless and until we acknowledge our fault and ask for forgiveness. I am glad.

Many of us are powerless in the face of the abuses we have suffered. It can appear that appalling people visit upon us dreadful things, and 'good' people suffer. One day God will judge all. No one will get away with anything. We will be called to account.

This helps me enormously. I am free to release what I can do nothing about. This does not discharge me from standing up for righteousness and justice. I am His voice on my small piece of earth.

Miroslav Volf talks about non-violence requiring a belief in God's wrath. When we know that any perpetrator of violence will not 'get away with it' and triumph eternally over their victim, we are free to rediscover that person's humanity and initiate God's love for them. Like Pope John Paul II who insisted on meeting with his failed assassin and his family. He forgave the man, lobbied for his pardon, and became a long-term family friend.

I remember discussing judgement and God's forgiveness and acceptance of anyone who asks for it with a friend. I knew about the coming to faith of various high-ranking Nazi officers through an unassuming prison chaplain called Henry Gerecke in Nuremburg. My friend could not accept that God's forgiveness was available even to those who had committed such horrific crimes. But that is God's promise to every single human being.

> For everyone who asks receives; he who seeks finds; and to him who knocks, the door will be opened.
> *Matthew 7:8*

Resurrection

> No eye has seen, no ear has heard, no mind has conceived what God has prepared for those who love him.
> *1 Corinthians 2:9*

When my husband's father died, his mother told him Albert had gone to be with Jesus. Steve was five years old, and he accepted it with his easy childlike faith. He doesn't remember mourning as his mother did. It was a catastrophic event for the family. Joyce now faced living a life she had not prepared for.

Death is the enemy to be overcome. Death was not God's original plan for us. Death is scary. King David, one of the psalmists in the Bible, never afraid to express his great vulnerability to God, wrote:

> My heart is in anguish within me;
> the terrors of death assail me.

Fear and trembling has beset me;
horror has overwhelmed me.
Psalm 55:4–5

We struggle when we lose fathers, mothers, children and loved ones by their dying too early, or, however old they are, too early for us. Death separates families; destroys relationships; causes mayhem, division and pain for countless human beings over the face of the earth. Death is the great leveller. 'Death is the destiny of every man; the living should take this to heart' (Ecclesiastes 7:2).

However much we fight, we will succumb. Accepting this truth presents the challenge of finding a pathway of peace. I found that pathway in God. Jesus said, 'I am the way and the truth and the life' (John 14:6). He is unique. He is the only person to have died and independently risen from the dead to be seen and recorded by many witnesses. God offers life to every single person who believes as we move from life, through death, into hope and resurrection.

Hope

Hope flutters
Like angel wings tapping on my shoulder –
Pain fanned by love.

What is our hope? Our hope is in a Person – He around whom all human history revolves.

Jesus was afraid in the Garden of Gethsemane. He was in such distress He sweated drops of actual blood, in horror of what was about happen to Him. (Sweating blood has a medical term: hematohidrosis, generally caused by acute fear and extreme stress.) A perfectly sane reason to be afraid. He faced an appalling death. Perhaps also His distress was in the act of dying. Something God had not yet experienced. He was prepared, out of His great love for humankind, to become like us *in every way*.

How did Jesus continue His journey? He called out to His Father for help. He submitted Himself to whatever God allowed with the words, 'yet not my will, but yours be done'.[39] Jesus' job was to destroy death by facing death head-on.

In approaching death, what we believe about God comes into sharp focus. What do you believe? Will your journey continue? 'There are no atheists in foxholes'.[40]

> To think death stops life is equivalent to thinking our moon defines the universe.

Appointment

If you don't know Him, let me urge you to look. It is never too late. Jesus said to the thief being crucified with Him after he asked Jesus to remember him, 'I tell you the truth, today you will be with me in paradise.'[41]

In a magazine article called 'Death the Enemy', Billy Graham writes about a columnist who suggested five things that ought to be done about death:

---

[39] Luke 22:42.
[40] Reverend William T. Cummings, www.conservapedia.com.
[41] Luke 23:43.

He said, 'First, accept the fact that you will die; second, make arrangements, if you are past 50 years, for the mechanics of dying; third, make provision for those you are leaving behind (check your insurance); fourth, make a will. Fifth,' he said, 'make an appointment with God, but I don't know how to suggest you do that.'[42]

How to make an appointment? We pray. We decide we want to know Him. If we take one small step towards Him, He will run to embrace us.

We must come to prayer humble and vulnerable with a soft repentant heart, for all the unworthy things we have done. Those not-God choices. Our focused determination to live a life revolving around ourselves. This is what the Bible calls sin.

If we don't recognise we need Him, God cannot help us.

One of the two thieves crucified alongside Jesus recognised that He was special. His encounter with Jesus was remarkable. He rebuked his fellow criminal with these words:

'Don't you fear God,' he said, 'since you are under the same sentence? We are punished justly, for we are getting what our deeds deserve. But this man has done nothing wrong.'

Then he said, 'Jesus, remember me when you come into your kingdom.'

[42] Billy Graham, 'Death the Enemy', 5th October 2009, Billy Graham Evangelistic Association (BGEA), http://www.billygraham.org.

Jesus answered him, 'I tell you the truth, today you will be with me in paradise.'
Luke 23:40–43

It is never too late.

A prayer to make your own

God, forgive me for all the things I choose to think and do
which are things You hate.
If you are real please reveal yourself to me. I invite You to
be part of my life.
Save me, heal my heart. Help me to love You and to
receive Your love for me.
Whatever time left of my life, I give it to You.
Help me to put right that which I can, and to receive Your
forgiveness
for that which I cannot.
May I understand Your grace and Your goodness forever
– in this life,
in my death, and fully in my new life.
Amen

Keep praying. If you prayed this prayer, find and tell someone who loves God. Ask that person to help you understand more.

Glory

Not only will we see Jesus when we die, or He comes again, but we will also share in Him as He truly is. Tom Wright in *Paul for Everyone: 2 Corinthians*[43] reminds us of the picture of an eclipse. We cannot look at an eclipse without a special covering for our eyes. Moses, after he met God face to face, had to wear a veil because his face shone with a brightness. In this life on earth, as we allow the Spirit to work in our lives, to heal us, mould us, teach us, lead us, God's glory touches our lives. By faith we can see this glory in the lives of those who love Him. However, there is the promise of more.

> When he appears, we shall be like him, for we shall see him as he is.
> *John 3:2*

> If the Scriptures didn't make it so plain, we wouldn't have the gall to make this up, even in our wildest dreams. But the apostle Paul tells us we 'will appear with him in glory' (Colossians 3:3), and that awaiting us is 'an eternal weight of glory' (2 Corinthians 4:16). Jesus himself prays to the Father about us, 'The glory that you have given me I have given to them' (John 17:22), and perhaps most shocking of all, Peter says we will 'become partakers of the divine nature' (2 Peter 1:4).
> *David Mathis*[44]

---

[43] Tom Wright, *Paul for Everyone: 2 Corinthians* (New Testament for Everyone) (London: SPCK, 2012).

[44] David Mathis, 'We Will Be Like Him', 28th June 2014, www.desiringGod.org.

The truth of such a promise appears impossible. Created in His image, both male and female.[45] Our status a little lower than the heavenly beings, or angels.[46] Jesus humbled Himself,[47] to become a human being, to change our destiny. Dying, perceived with dread as the worst event, becomes the greatest moment of our life as we step through the portal into glory.

Paul, as always, puts it perfectly.

> The sufferings of this present time are not worth comparing with the glory that is to be revealed to us.
> *Romans 8:18 (ESV)*

Paul suffered immensely for the gospel. He did not appear to blame God. He must have questioned at times, when the journey was hard, whether he followed God's will, but he never faltered. His relentless pursuit of giving away the Good News to all remains a powerful model. A learned man, a Jewish rabbi of passion and determination and fierce integrity, yet after he met Jesus on the Damascus Road,[48] he was compelled to reconfigure his entire construct of faith. He was an extraordinary human being.

I think it fitting that we give the apostle Paul the final word about resurrection:

> Listen, I tell you a mystery: We will not all sleep, but we will all be changed – in a flash, in the twinkling of an eye, at the last trumpet. For the trumpet will

---

[45] Genesis 1:27.

[46] Psalm 8:5.

[47] Philippians 2:8.

[48] Acts 9:1–19.

sound, the dead will be raised imperishable, and we will be changed. For the perishable must clothe itself with the imperishable, and the mortal with immortality. When the perishable has been clothed with the imperishable, and the mortal with immortality, then the saying that is written will come true: 'Death has been swallowed up in victory.'

1 Corinthians 15:51–54

The journey continues but you are not alone. Allow yourself to experience the presence of the One who has gone before.

I love this poem by Rosy Prue,[49] a wonderfully creative and beautiful lady. Enjoy.

How to Fly
by Rosy Prue

Just lean back,
Close your eyes and let go.
Trust me.
I won't let you down.
Feel me behind you, around you,
Holding you up.
My power is more tangible than the wind,
Warmer than the sun.
Feel it soar around you,
Feel it beat upon your face

---

[49] Rosy Prue, artist and arts education consultant, www.rosyprue.com.

Sway – dizzy-headed but safe
No tension in your being
Buffeted by the waves of my love.
Lean into me – I will support you
Lean forward – I will catch you
Lean backwards – I will be there
Lean sideways balance on the currents of air
As I breathe on you
I WILL NOT LET YOU FALL.
Lift your face to meet my kiss
Reach and I will lift you
Up, where the wind will roar in your ears, play with your
hair
Up, where the sunlight bathes
Gliding, soaring, spinning
Trust me
I WILL NOT LET YOU FALL.

Chapter 4
Emotional Health –
Communicating with Ourselves
and Our Loved Ones

Connect

Connection between the person who accepts they are dying and their loving friends and relatives is essential.

> I define connection as the energy that exists between people when they feel seen, heard, and valued; when they can give and receive without judgment; and when they derive sustenance and strength from the relationship.
> *Dr Brené Brown*[50]

You need to find others to journey with and, equally, allow yourself to be found. We are social creatures. We crave companionship, we need friendship, and one danger of pain is we can disconnect from others. We can turn inward and gnaw away at ourselves. This can then lead to a growing depression and despair. Anger may rise within you as it did for Dylan Thomas who raged in his poem, 'Do

---

[50] Brené Brown, *The Gifts of Imperfection* (Center City, MN: Hazelden Publishing, 2010).

Not Go Gentle into That Good night'.[51] Whatever your emotional state sharing the journey with others is essential.

This can be a wonderfully intimate and affirming time. Speak the unspoken out loud, perhaps for the first time. How healthy if everything can be placed on the table. Questions asked about family history. Questions about long-term puzzlements can lift their head above the parapet. Openness, honesty and vulnerability in both the listener and the one being listened to are rare and beauteous gifts. Now is the time to share.

This can either be a fear-filled, awkward and embarrassing time or, at its best, a joy-filled period of intimate connection.

We may worry that we will say the wrong things and make things worse. We might decide to leave it to the professionals. We will miss the intimacy of heart-to-heart connection. Pretending people will recover when the prognosis for the illness is terminal misses all the possibilities for connection, understanding, tenderness and affection. We are programmed with an instinctive desire to hold tenaciously on to life. However, death inhabits our world and all, without exception, will face it.

If we have not confronted our own fear of death, then we will struggle to establish healthy relationships. We will be an ineffective companion to talk and to listen to our loved one.

Long suppressed feelings of anger, shame or regret may well surface. These should be allowed and heard.

---

[51] Dylan Thomas, 'Do Not Go Gentle into That Good Night', www.poets.org.

Strong feelings of not wanting to upset or be a burden to our family and friends can bubble up and create disquiet. Issues regarding trust because of our life experiences can thwart our resolve. Dismiss such thoughts and determine to connect.

Emotions charge through us, but tears need to flow. We don't need to be sorted out, to have answers, to understand. In facing death together, hand holding hand, love and care creates a tender and compassionate bridge. We need space to say goodbye with or without words. It is essential for everyone involved, including children.

Privacy is important. It is problematic to find intimacy in a hospital ward, but not impossible. We are creative people, we can find creative solutions – ask for help.

We can pray together. 'For where two or three come together in my name, there am I with them' (Matthew 18:20).

Connection allows us to continue to grow, to produce good positive fruit in our lives.

Connect through play

We may not look or feel our best, but fun and laughter are an essential ingredient to well-being. While you are still alive, live. While life and death are a serious business, at whatever stage, learn to play a little more. 'You can discover more about a person in an hour of play than in a year of conversation' (Plato).[52]

---

[52] www.brainyquote.com.

While the benefits of play for children as they grow are well documented, adults often find it difficult to continue to play. Perhaps we found it a chore to play with our children. Most of us believe we are too busy to play. Yet play can bring a huge amount of joy into our lives and contribute to our sense of mental and emotional well-being.

When I imagine play, I might want to chuck snowballs, but play incorporates a number of things. Going to the theatre, art, books, music, comedy programmes, daydreaming, board games, cards, dance, throwing a ball, but it is hard to define. It's not usually about accomplishing a goal but about being, enjoying something that is fun and pleasurable. At its best, play involves someone else.

We are changing, though. Some of the best-selling books at the moment are adult colouring books. For my husband and myself, one thing we love to do is play cards, particularly on holiday. We sit in a restaurant with a view, order a drink and play cards. We 'hang out'. We chat. It is a hugely companionable time which continues between food courses. For a change, time doesn't matter and we simply enjoy each other's company.

Stuart Brown MD compares play to oxygen. He writes, 'It's all around us, yet goes mostly unnoticed or unappreciated until it is missing.'[53]

---

[53] Stuart Brown MD with Christopher Vaughan, *Play: How It Shapes the Brain, Opens the Imagination and Invigorates the Soul* (New York: J. P. Tarcher / Penguin Putnam, 2010).

Dancing with the feet is one thing, but dancing with the heart is another.[54]

Dancing makes me bask in the sun and worship.

On social media, we see film of a person who begins to sing in a train carriage. They hand out song sheets to a familiar song. The single instrumentalist strums a few chords and before the song ends, many embarrassed and unsure people who joined in are now are smiling, talking to their neighbour, having had an enjoyable, life-enhancing experience. I love watching them. That's play.

Why not …

- Compile a fun bucket list. Anything you long to do?

- Choose a drawer and fill it with things that you find fun. When things become difficult, oppressive, and depressive, open the drawer and take out something to play with. This could be Lego, Play-Doh, a calligraphy set, a jigsaw puzzle, baking utensils, embroidery, a train set … the list is endless.

- Your idea.

You could reignite the child inside and allow a sense of joy to spill out. You are never too old to play or too ill to enjoy watching others, joining in with a smile. Play can be part of living your best life.

---

[54] Author unknown. Available at www.quotes.thinkexist.com (last visited 9th June 2017).

'I tell you the truth, unless you change and become like little children, you will never enter the kingdom of heaven. Therefore, whoever humbles himself like this child is the greatest in the kingdom of heaven.'
Matthew 18:3–4

Suicide

Fear can be the driver behind the increasing pressure for euthanasia or assisted suicide. Most British adults in the ComRes[55] statistics stated the most important thing for a good death was to be pain-free. Fear of suffering, of dependence, of medical overtreatment means some of us look to control exactly how we die.

Professor John Wyatt writes:

Euthanasia is intentional killing, by act or omission, of a person whose life is thought not to be worth living. This is not the same as:

- Withdrawing medical treatment which is futile or burdensome, or where the patient is 'actively dying'. This is good medical care.

- Giving pain-killing treatment in order to benefit the patient which may have the unintended side effect of shortening life. This is the principle of double effect – recognising

55 ComRes interview. See note 23.

the   difference   between   intention   and
foresight.[56]

Doctor-assisted suicide is also intentional medical killing but the final act is performed by the patient.

My father and my stepmother died in Holland within a few months of each other. My father died at home, my stepmother in hospital. In the Netherlands, euthanasia by doctors is legal in cases of 'hopeless and unbearable' suffering. My stepmother was dying of heart failure. I struggled to orientate myself to the fact she asked the doctors to end her life in the midst of a distressing and painful illness. She put her affairs in order. We remained with her in hospital until she took her final breath in the early hours of the morning.

With good hospice care, palliative care, specialist end-of-life nursing either at home or in hospital, and clear forward thinking, much is now available. Medical care at its best can allow for a peaceful, reverent, holistic death.

My mother was taken into hospital in the UK and diagnosed with an obstructed bowel. The ensuing operation took a surprising seven hours, and she failed to regain consciousness afterwards. Unable to breathe by herself, she had a respirator attached. After seven days the staff changed her care to assisted-breathing via a tracheotomy. If she did wake she would not be able to speak. My sisters and I knew she would absolutely hate to

[56] Professor John Wyatt, *Matters of Life & Death* (Leicester: IVP, New Edition 2010, 2011, 2012). From Seminar 1 at Spring Harvest, July 2015, 'Dying Well and Dying Faithfully – Issues at the End of Life'.

remain like this, but she had not written an Advance Decision (see 'Practicalities'). I was delegated to talk to the doctors. We anticipated a difficult conversation.

On the tenth day she woke, completely in charge of her faculties. Although she couldn't speak because of the tracheotomy, she indicated clearly what she wanted. I spoke to her, outlining her situation. According to the doctors, she would always need a respirator. Without it she would die. I asked her if she wished the assisted breathing to continue. She shook her head – no.

We talked to the doctor. He interviewed her with a nurse and ourselves present. Her responses made it obvious she did not wish to live with a respirator. We agreed this was her choice. He gently explained to her that they could increase her medication and gradually reduce the respirator. There would be no pain, no discomfort. Again she indicated her assent to the decision. That night she died exactly as he had explained. It was peaceful, we remained with her, softly talking to her or stroking her arm, and we could say goodbye. She was eighty years old.

Steps can be taken where you make positive decisions and remain in control of your end-of-life care through your appointed attorneys and those named in your Advance Decision. (See 'Lasting Power of Attorney' and 'Advance Decision' in 'Practicalities'.)

Heart health

Never succumb to the temptation of bitterness.
Dr Martin Luther King Jr[57]

How is your heart?

How truthful are you prepared to be with yourself?

Have you stored up anything that is corrosive not only to yourself but also to others?

If you imagine your heart as a harbour, what boats have you allowed to moor and take up residence?

Boats with names like bitterness and unforgiveness, pride, resentment. If these things are given a berth in your heart, they will hurt you far more than they hurt the other person.

> When the root is bitterness, imagine what the fruit might be.
> *Dr Woodrow Kroll*[58]

The choice is yours. Keep them tethered in your life or decide to deal with each boat and sink them in the depths of the ocean.

It is easy to accommodate rubbish. We dismiss it with 'Oh, we don't talk any more'; 'I'm waiting for them to speak to me first'; 'They hurt me so much'; 'It was so unfair'; 'I will never speak to them again.'

---

[57] Dr Martin Luther King Jr, www.brainyquote.com.
[58] Dr Woodrow Kroll, preacher and radio host, USA, 'A Root of Bitterness' in Lessons on Living, www.backtothebible.org.

These unresolved issues eat away inside us. You say to yourself, 'I've tried; there is nothing more I can do; I can't face the pain; it's too late.'

Bitterness begins as hurt from someone you perceive has abused and wronged you. Anger and resentment grow. Hurt feelings are nursed and rehearsed. Time passes and ugliness and pain establish themselves within you.

Bitterness cannot stay in a neat box. With time it infects our whole life. The more we feed it, the more it grows. Eventually unpleasantness pervades everything we do and say. We become its victim.

It manifests itself in anxiety and/or depression. It pollutes our attitudes with distrust and cynicism. Centimetre by centimetre our lives fill with pessimism, a sense of futility and unhappiness. Unresolved issues make us ill. Connection with others becomes more and more difficult.

> I know from personal experience how damaging it can be to live with bitterness and unforgiveness. I like to say it's like taking poison and hoping your enemy will die. And it really is that harmful to us to live this way.
> Joyce Meyer[59]

This is not a way to live or to die. No medication can relieve the disquiet of such negative thoughts and emotions.

---

[59] Joyce Meyer, 'Do Yourself a Favour … Forgive', an interview with Joyce Meyer, www.cbn.com.

We all make mistakes. Most people, particularly our loved ones, do not want to hurt us. (I accept some terrible wrongs and horrific abuses happen that are not our fault. This is not what I am talking about. However, even in circumstances of extreme violation, forgiveness will set us free.)

We do not want to live with the pain of broken relationships, but we don't know what to do.

Perhaps if we go back to the perceived wrong and imagine ourselves in the shoes of the 'wrongdoer', we might find a truth that will liberate us.

It requires humility to go to a person, to talk, reconcile and ultimately find peace together. Sometimes we need an empathetic third party. Be brave and bold enough to take the steps and let go of resentment, bitterness and anger. The aftermath will bring emotional, physical and mental release. You will discover compassion, understanding, relief and peace.

I remember my son as an older teenager admitting he had worried all day because he thought I was angry with him. I didn't remember the incident, but was shocked at my power. This boy I loved with my whole heart had spent a day in disquiet. It taught me a great lesson.

I grew up steeped in emotional blackmail and my resolution was never to allow it in my family. In our home, if issues occurred, the aim was to resolve them as quickly as possible. We wanted no undercurrent of emotion hovering over the family.

The pain my son carried through only strengthened my resolve. He had misunderstood me, but I still apologised. Peace returned to him and I interrogated my behaviour.

Forgiveness is always possible even if reconciliation is not. Forgiveness is a difficult, quality decision, not a feeling. A decision that will take time to process.

If you are the person who needs forgiveness, then humility is required to talk about your regret and sorrow without excuse. So much healing in relationship is contained within the simple word 'Sorry'. Humility is about service to others, not fixating on yourself.

If you forgive or ask for forgiveness, then you free not only those you have tethered, but also yourself.

Humility gives value to every person it meets.

First, ask forgiveness from God for your lack of forgiveness, even if you are the abused one. His forgiveness will then give you the strength to forgive or ask forgiveness from the person.

As you reflect on forgiveness, allow yourself space to forgive yourself. A raging sense of guilt can hit you. Peace can be found.

> For all have sinned and fall short of the glory of God, and are justified freely by his grace through the redemption that came by Christ Jesus.
> *Romans 3:23–24*

The second greatest commandment that Jesus taught His disciples was to 'Love your neighbour as yourself' (Mark 12:31).

We hear the words to love others, but we struggle to love ourselves. Many of us suffer from cripplingly low self-esteem. Actions we regret are often born out of the need to shore up that self-esteem.

I was a special needs teacher. Tasked one day with teaching a class of six-year-olds, we studied together the Great Fire of London. They were a dynamic and enjoyable class. I kept complimenting them on their work. They worked so hard I decided to release them early for their afternoon playtime. Also, every child in the class would receive a sticker. Great excitement ensued. They lined up to go outside. I walked the line, giving each child a sticker. They were proud and delighted – until I got to Gemma.

Gemma refused to let me put a sticker on her. I asked her to wait while I stickered all the other children and they disappeared to play. Puzzled, I asked Gemma why she didn't want her reward. I reminded her of her achievements. She deserved a sticker. Still she shook her head. Eventually she mumbled, 'I don't deserve one.' I could have wept.

This dear child had so little self-esteem that even receiving a sticker was too much for her. It took time, but we got there. She skipped out of the classroom, proud to display her own sticker. One of the best moments of my life.

What do we do to each other? Why do we believe we deserve so little?

Our culture likes to undermine people rather than build them up. There is no one I have met who didn't need encouragement and affirmation.

I have been a Street Pastor for the past seven years. One of our aims is to give value to every single person we meet. It is an honour to do so.

Regret – finding what is lost

We have one life. We make many decisions which fit somewhere on a continuum between good and bad. The older we get, the more we look back. If this disturbs your peace, fills you with sadness, then why not write down what is worrying you? Afterwards, find a trusted confidante with whom you can share intimately. You will find it releasing and empowering.

Jesus tells many parables in the Bible about loss. These wonderful stories were designed to make His hearers reflect again on things they thought they understood. Jesus loved to unsettle the comfortable with His wisdom.

There are three stories of loss: the lost sheep, the lost coin and the lost son.[60] Wise words have been said regarding these three; however, there is one new thought to me that I owe to Amy-Jill Levine in her book *Short Stories by Jesus*.[61] The shepherd who lost the sheep, the woman who lost the coin and the father who lost the son all had a responsibility to find what they had lost.

Shad Ali, an ex-social worker, is a British Pakistani who has lived and worked in Nottingham all his life. In July 2008 while riding his bike, he heard the racial abuse of two Pakistani women. He dismounted and tried to intervene.

---

[60] Luke 15:4–32.

[61] Amy-Jill Levine, *Short Stories by Jesus* (London: Bravo Ltd, 2015).

He was punched to the ground and a man stamped on and kicked his face repeatedly. He was hospitalised, receiving major reconstructive surgery to his face. It caused months of physical pain and psychological and emotional trauma.

His assailant was arrested and received a five-year custodial sentence.

Shad Ali,[62] though, rejected the retribution argued for by his friends, unable to conceive of inflicting on another what had happened to him. He wanted to forgive. What follows is an excerpt from his account:

> I received a huge amount of criticism and confusion from friends and family who didn't understand why I wanted to forgive – especially from my wife who initially felt nothing but hatred towards this man. In spite of this, forgiving has really helped me move forward after the attack. It has been about me and has nothing to do with the man who attacked me. And yet, from the beginning, I wanted more than anything to meet my attacker.
>
> After years of persisting with my request to visit him, I was finally allowed to exchange letters with him, and I found out that he was full of remorse and wanted to meet me, too.
>
> I tried not to have any expectations of what the day would bring. Once we shook hands, we spontaneously hugged, which was totally unexpected, and I became very emotional and started crying. During the conference we shared our individual experiences from the day of the attack

---

[62] Shad Ali, www.theforgivenessproject.com.

and also a bit of our life stories. By the end of the meeting, it felt like we had become friends.

Both men had lost a great deal in the violence. Shad Ali was brave enough to work for reconciliation.

Alone with my mother as she lay dying in hospital, I asked her if she would like me to pray with her. She nodded assent, as she could not speak. I was shocked, but it became another great moment in my life. I loved a God who loved her unconditionally. I knew with certainty He would embrace her if she reached out to Him.

Why had life been so difficult between my mother and me? I never understood. When I became a God-lover I determined that I would always reach out to her, however difficult, and as she got older we managed a probationary relationship.

However, after the funeral and celebration of her life, I began to get ill. I recognised the root as unresolved things in my relationship with her. Fortunately, my father, who had died four years before, was a hoarder. Among his things were all the letters my mother had written to him. These dated from before their marriage in 1948 until their divorce in 1964. I declined to read them while my mother was alive. Now I took them on holiday with my husband for a week in the New Forest with our bikes. A routine was established. I would rise early, read a couple of letters and take notes. As we rode around the New Forest, I would regale my husband with all I had learned that day. He listened, interested and engaged, as I worked my way through my growing years. It was healing. I came back well, refreshed, having learned a great deal about my past, and at peace with my mother.

What was the biggest thing I learned?

How fickle memory is. What I think I remember is not *the* truth, it is *a* truth I have distorted to fit with my view of myself and others. Laying down my own distortions in order to embrace reconciliation will reap the most wholesome fruit.

Jesus went on and on about love. The New Testament goes on and on about love. Love, as described in 1 Corinthians 13:4-7,[63] is everything.

Love never gives up.
Love cares more for others than for self.
Love doesn't want what it doesn't have.
Love doesn't strut,
Doesn't have a swelled head,
Doesn't force itself on others,
Isn't always 'me first,'
Doesn't fly off the handle,
Doesn't keep score of the sins of others,
Doesn't revel when others grovel,
Takes pleasure in the flowering of truth,
Puts up with anything,
Trusts God always,
Always looks for the best,
Never looks back,
But keeps going to the end.

---

[63] *The Message*.

Thankfulness

I never met a bitter person who was thankful. Or a
thankful person who was bitter.
Nick Vujicic[64]

Be thankful for your life. Living with a sense of gratitude
is life-enhancing not only for yourself, but also for those
near you. A thankful person is a delight to be around.

You might say, 'How can I be thankful in this situation?'
Open your eyes, what do you see? It may surprise you.

There is a calmness to a life lived in gratitude and
quiet joy.
Ralph H. Blum[65]

God is good. He doesn't change. He will not stop loving
us. He promises not to leave us.[66] He is faithful. Most of our
difficulties arise from the fact we do not trust Him.
Cultivate a thankful heart, whatever the circumstances.
This is not failure to face reality; this is not pretending
everything will work out well; this is not denying an all-
encompassing grief.

God will be with us every step of our journey.

He will encompass us with His love.

Nothing can or will separate us from Him.[67]

Love listens, love hears, love waits, love brings peace that passes understanding.[68]

Depression

It is understandable that sadness, dejection, wretchedness overwhelm you as you face loss. However, despair and debilitating melancholy arising from grief could mean a logical reaction morphs into clinical depression.

'My God, my God, why have you forsaken me?'
Matthew 27:46

The words of Jesus as He hung on the cross recognise the depth of human suffering. He did not separate Himself from your pain. He experienced unimaginable depths of agony like you, and for a time felt crushingly isolated.

Signs of a clinical depression include all enjoyment disappearing from activities you normally relished. You find yourself withdrawing from the life-enhancing relationships of friends and family. This may occur because of your primary illness, and/or certain medications and treatments you are taking. Ask the medical people caring for you about what side-effects might occur with your particular prescriptions. Medications work differently with different people. There is treatment available for clinical depression. If you think you or your loved one is suffering, do not hesitate to seek medical help.

---

[68] Philippians 4:7.

Anxiety and sadness can be improved by talking to someone and receiving the appropriate help. Seek a support group.[69] If travel is difficult, try an online support group. Failure to talk to at least one person will only accentuate your unhappiness and isolation. Remember to be kind to yourself, take yourself seriously and ask for help.

I understand it is difficult to know how to broach the subject of dying and death. It took all my courage to begin the conversation with my father. He remained the very private man he had always been. Now I would take a different approach. The following is helpful:

- Listen carefully. Is there anything to latch on to in order to help you talk?

- Ask them to help you cope with their death by talking about their wishes, eg funeral music, burial.

- Is there anyone they would like to see or contact if they become seriously ill?

- What would they like you to do if they become ill? Read to them, sit with them?[70]

If you have no language to talk about dying and death, dive in and learn to swim together. Remember relatives

---

[69] Living with Dying Self-Help and Support Group, www.dyingmatters.org; support information and help groups related to helping patients face death and dying, www.patient.info.
[70] Information gathered including 'Talking about Death and Dying', www.dyingmatters.org.

and friends need talk-time alongside the person who is dying.

You are a beginner, you will say the wrong thing. You can always apologise. 'Sorry' is the most wonderful word. You can start again. You will improve. Always assure people that you love and value them.

Secrets

Secrets lock away the heart
and you become
the person you never meant to be.

There are many reasons we keep secrets in our lives, power or protection being two. Historically, difficult things occurring within the family were often kept secret.

Secrets lock away the heart.

For example, my unmarried great-aunt gave birth to a child. A photograph of the child, though sent for adoption, was hidden by my great-grandmother behind a photo of her daughter. She kept this on her bedside cabinet. She never told her husband or anyone else in the family.

The baby was my great-aunt's only child.

Years later, in the late nineties, her daughter found her. Now married with three children of her own, she wanted to meet her birth mother – a tremendous gift to my great-aunt in her latter years as she embraced the role of grandmother within a family that accepted and loved her.

Nowadays we think secrets should be unlocked. Sharing them needs careful thought, at the right time and place. As we journey towards death, questions long buried should be allowed to surface. A powerful dividing force disturbing the equilibrium of a family can, by truth-telling, bring freedom into relationships damaged through lack of trust and intimacy. Such openness can release and heal families. Love may flourish and revelation and understanding allow those whose lives continue to blossom in a new way.

Dying is not only about yourself, but also about those you leave.

Encouragement

> Encourage someone
> and for that moment
> watch them bask in the sun.

Have you been an encourager of others in your life? All of us need and thrive on encouragement. British society loves to pull people down, to reduce them. We are afraid of praise. We fear if you praise people they will 'get too big for their boots' or 'their heads will swell'. Maybe that is true; however, for most of us our self-worth is low and always needs boosting.

In your family, were you someone who praised or criticised? Did you encourage or discourage? I have a friend who struggles to speak encouragement to their children or friends. Their father never praised them and they find it extremely difficult to praise others.

Don't assume the children, parents, friends, family around you know what they mean to you. If you cannot say the words, then write them. Write to those special ones and leave it with your will. After your death they may bask in the love and appreciation that you had for them. Say thank you. Remember an instance when love for them touched you. Think of a moment of success of which you were proud, and praise them for it.

Leave a legacy of applause that will live long in the hearts of your loved ones.

Chapter 5
Counselling/Guidance

As a learner you are in uncharted territory when you are face to face with your imminent mortality. Lifted bodily off your feet, as if by a tornado, you have been deposited in an alien country. Think of Dorothy in *The Wizard of Oz*. Do not be surprised if equilibrium is lost. Now is the time you need support, companionship and encouragement. You might consider taking advantage of some professional counselling.

I hope this did not happen – however, if you received the news of your diagnosis alone, revisit with a companion to hear it again. The sense of shock may mean you didn't ask all the questions.

If you love God, then see your spiritual leader – a minister/pastor, a leader in the church. You will need help: spiritual guidance, support through the stages of grief, and prayer. Ask your church to pray for you.

It is important to strike a balance between the natural prognosis of our illness and faith. Prayer for healing is important. God heals, but we will need a spiritual preparation for the fact we may not recover. This is not a lack of faith. Rather it is the prayer of Mary when she hears the message from the angel Gabriel, 'let it be to me according to your word'.[71]

I interviewed two professionals, both chaplains to a cancer hospital.[72] They agreed one of the most difficult deaths to witness was the death of someone who refused to accept the prognosis, certain God would heal them.

They cited a young Christian man. Convinced of God's healing, he would brook no discussion on the possibility of death. His church bolstered him in his 'faith'. A lost opportunity for his loved ones to say goodbye. In their view it was heart-breaking.

Death isn't just about the person who dies, it is about those that remain alive, too. Also, we will miss out on their affirmation, love and prayers, as we slip into the presence of God.

A few sessions one-to-one with a trained counsellor[73] can be of enormous benefit to help us find the words for what is happening to us. They will not be emotionally involved, will have a very honest approach, and can help us overcome our reticence and fear about words like 'dying' and 'death'. This affords an excellent preparation to talk to our close family and friends. Some GP surgeries

---

[71] Luke 1:38, ESV.

[72] Rev Angie Tunstall, chaplain, The Christie NHS Foundation Trust; Rev Andrew Bradley, chaplain, The Christie NHS Foundation Trust.

[73] www.itsgoodtotalk.org.uk/therapists (British Association of Counsellors and Psychotherapists), www.psychotherapy.org.uk (UK Council for Psychotherapy). Select: Find a Therapist.

can help with counsellors. Other counselling services offer a 'pay-what-you-can' deal.

The chaplains I spoke to both testified to the fact that massage, aromatherapy and other complementary and alternative therapies now available can be wonderfully relaxing and calming.

When we come to where we want to talk with friends and family, we might need to recognise that we must be the brave one.

- *Choose the right time* – uninterrupted, as we will want to allow for silence and questions.

- *Choose the right place* – without disturbance.

- *Ask questions* – 'I know it will be hard but do you think we should speak about what's going to happen?'

- *Listen* – it might still be too challenging, so change the subject: 'OK, that's fine, but I do hope we can talk about it another time as this is something that would really help me.'

Listening well means being present in every moment of a conversation. Do not interrupt. Do not finish sentences. Do not fill in spaces or silences. Do not allow your mind to wander or daydream. Listen to the answers given. Do not decide what the answers should be.

When I am there to listen, I will often have a notebook with me and take a few notes. It keeps me on-task. It helps us both if the thread of the conversation is lost as I can remind the speaker where they got to. It is also helpful when we pick up the conversation at a later date to remind both of us what we discussed. If either of us had agreed on a task, it can serve as a reminder.

Don't be afraid of emotion – ours or theirs.[74]

Facing the news of terminal illness in a loved one

The shock of the news will have been the equivalent of an earthquake to the family. Everyone will have a different coping mechanism. If the family is used to expressing emotion and dealing with it positively, then there is opportunity to support each other, understanding the shared fears and worries. Some of us function differently. We receive news and we lock it down inside us. This creates a difficulty as pressure builds inside and eventually explodes in us. We get sick, we have accidents, we burst out in anger or other damaging emotions. All of us need to find ways to share feelings, and what we are going through.

If we are God-lovers, we will want to see our spiritual leader to bring wisdom, guidance and encouragement and to pray with us. If we belong to churches, we will want them to pray for our loved one and our family.

Everyone will have to find a way to adjust to the changing roles in the family. Things will feel unbalanced and out of sync for a long while, especially if it is the perceived 'head' of the family who is dying. It could be useful to think about getting a family counsellor to visit a few times to help the expression of pain and to enable

[74] Information gathered from websites, see 'Further help'.

good, positive communication with each other. Remember, we are all learners at this. We are not supposed to know what to do.

Another place where help is available is the hospice. Doing this sooner rather than later can be incredibly supportive for everyone. The mission of a hospice is to help the dying die with comfort, dignity and love, and to help family and friends to cope both before and after the death. This is not a lack of faith, it is wise preparation.

Practical help is a good place to start, especially if talking is too difficult. Order the food shopping to arrive on the doorstep. Deliver meals for the freezer. Hire a cleaner. Ask the church for help. Pray together. Read Scripture together. Go on outings together.

Take time to live while there is still life.

Further help

www.dyingmatters.org: This site has well thought-through information on all matters of death and bereavement. One particular section is called Find Me Help. Simply punch in your postcode to uncover an array of possible places near you. I did so and immediately ten sites came up, including a hospital, a hospice, two bereavement care homes, a carers' centre and several Age UK bases. They also have an Advanced Search with different categories to enlarge the scope of what is on offer. There are other sites:

www.healthtalk.org
www.counselling-directory.org.uk

www.griefwords.com
www.rcpsych.ac.uk
www.ageuk.org.uk
www.deathisnotdying.com
www.Ata**Loss**.org

Spiritual

Sixty-four per cent of people rank having their religious/spiritual needs met as the least important need in having a 'good death' out of the options tested.[75] Our spiritual needs are much more important than we think.

Perhaps our faith has been a quiet thing inside us. We don't belong to a church, or know any Christians. Nothing will ever disqualify us from the God who loves us, but we will need help. There are some wonderful people ordained into a variety of faith establishments whose experience in listening, caring and helping can be enormously beneficial. In the hospital or hospice, there will be faith representatives, ie chaplains. If we are at home, there will be churches where a minister would be only too glad to call and give whatever help they can. We simply need to ask.

All can and will offer prayer. Some will bring communion to us if we wish it. They would be only too delighted to bring spiritual help and faith, and minister the peace of God to the carers, the friends, the family and the person who is dying. They 'feed the soul' in a way that should not be ignored or forgotten.

---

[75] ComRes interview. See note 23.

We don't have to walk alone

We are all learners at saying goodbye.

But goodbye is not the end of the story for those who love God. We can rail at our situation. We can shout, 'Why me?' The truth is, why not us? This world is a world groaning for release into the new heaven and new earth that will be made manifest when we are resurrected. Bad things happen in this imperfect world.

While we might be dying, or facing the death of a loved one earlier that we think we should, we will all die. God always appears good to us when things are going well, not when everything appears to be falling apart. We can't make God into someone we want Him to be. God will be whom God will be. One day we will understand.

What if we were to live each day with the knowledge of our imminent death? Would it radically change our perspective?

I remember at eighteen years old looking for something that made sense of the world in which I found myself.

- Was I supposed to make money?

- Was I supposed to try to become famous?

- Was it about freedom, about sex, about self-gratification?

Whatever we give our heart to is what owns us. The Bible puts it so much better.

> Do not store up for yourselves treasure on earth, where moth and rust destroy, and where thieves

> break in and steal ... For where your treasure is,
> there your heart will be also.
> *Matthew 6:19, 21*

I found a Person who loved me. He gave me a gift. There was nothing I could do to make Him love me more, and nothing I could do to make Him love me less.

I, too, am dying, like you are because I am a human being. But that, of course, is not the end of my story, nor the end of your story.

> We know that God, who raised the Lord Jesus, will also raise us with Jesus and present us to himself together with you ...
> That is why we never give up. Though our bodies are dying, our spirits are being renewed every day. For our present troubles are small and won't last very long. Yet they produce for us a glory that vastly outweighs them and will last forever! So we don't look at the troubles we can see now; rather, we fix our gaze on things that cannot be seen. For the things we see now will soon be gone, but the things we cannot see will last forever.
> *2 Corinthians 4:14, 16–18 (NLT)*

This book is a beginner's guide and therefore the second half concentrates on the practicalities we have to face regarding our estate and ourselves when we die.

There are questions to be asked regarding your will. Why should you make one? How do you make one? What is legal? What is the entirety of your estate? What will you pass on to family and friends? Are there letters you need to write?

Do you know how you wish to be cared for at the end of your life? There are several legal ways to do this. What information is important for your family and your carers to know?

Do you have firm views regarding your funeral? What are your preferences to include in the Celebration of Life event? What is your favourite music, your much-loved poem or excerpt from a book? Who is your choice to officiate? Who would you ask to participate?

Where would you wish to be buried? You will be surprised by the options available.

You are not yet dead, therefore now is the time to live. There will be choices available to you. Anyone you wish to see? A particular place to visit or revisit?

Take your time. You don't have to address everything all in one go. It might appear a mountain to climb, but climbing it will bring a sense of peace and order.

> If Jesus Christ was really raised from the dead – if he is really the Son of God and you believe in him – all these things that you long for most desperately will come true at last.
>
> We will escape time and death.
>
> We will know love without parting, we will even communicate with non-human beings (angels) and we will see evil defeated forever … all those longings will be fulfilled in real time, space, and history.
>
> *Tim Keller*[76]

---

[76] Tim Keller, *Making Sense of God* (New York: Viking, 2016).

PART TWO

PRACTICALITIES

Still silent body
But within my spirit sings
Dancing in love-light.
Abigail Witchalls[77]

---

[77] Abigail Witchalls as she lay, paralysed but smiling, in her hospital bed, the survivor of a knife attack, carrying a child in her womb, dictated – through blinking eyes – this haiku.

Chapter 6
Leaving with Order

Wills

Writing a will

We all fear death.

Seventy per cent of us say we are comfortable talking about death, but most haven't drawn up wills, discussed end-of-life wishes or put funeral plans in place.

We live in an age of ever-more complicated financial affairs and intricate family relationships. The numbers of us who make a will have dropped from 39 per cent (2009) to 35 per cent (2013).[78]

The treasury gains millions of pounds from people who die intestate – without a will.

Making a will is not morbid.

Making a will does not mean we are about to die.

I empathise with feeling unnerved about this subject. Thoughts of my own dying and death have swirled around in my imagination and dreams since beginning to write this book. I began to wonder whether somehow, deep

---

[78] Janet Shucksmith, Sarit Carlebach and Vicki Whittaker, 'British Social Attitudes (BSA) NatCen Social Research-Discussing & Planning for End of Life', March 2015, www.bsa.natcen.ac.uk.

down, I knew I would die soon, and this was my way of preparing for it.

If we are near our end-of-life journey, then making a will is an absolute necessity, not only for us but, crucially, for those we love.

We can make a will using a solicitor, or we can do-it-yourself online.

Making our will – using a solicitor

1. They will afford protection should there be a problem when it is read.

2. They will help us think forensically about every eventuality and scenario and what provision we might wish to make.

3. They will ensure it is legal, clear and any updates are validated correctly and free from possible contestation.

4. They are more expensive, but expert advice could be a wise investment.

5. Using a professional makes it self-evident that the will has been drawn up voluntarily, by a person of sound mind without any sense of coercion.

6. They will ensure accuracy.

7. They will ensure specificity in the distribution of assets.

8. They will make sure it is witnessed correctly. If a beneficiary witnesses your will they would be unable to inherit anything.

Making our will – online

1. A will can be made without a solicitor online from any number of websites which will take us step-by-step through the process.

    *   The fee is usually cheaper than a solicitor.

    *   It can be instantly printed on a home printer.

    *   It can be stored online.

    *   We can make unlimited updates, usually free.

2. Validation: the will and each and every update will need to be signed in the presence of witnesses (who cannot be beneficiaries).

3. Accuracy is paramount: names of people, of charities, of any beneficiary should be spelt correctly to avoid doubt or any possibility of contestation.

4. Distribution of assets should be as specific as possible. No one can ask us to clarify what we meant when we are dead.

5. A solicitor could then be used to assess what we have done and assure legality.

Wills[79] and generosity

It is important to write your will while you are of sound mind.

---

[79] The Money Advice Service (GB), 'Making a will and planning what to leave', www.moneyadviceservice.org.uk.

Why not do this as soon as you acquire any assets, whatever your age?

Choose executors with care. It is they who will collate all the assets, deal with the paperwork, and pay all the debts, taxes and funeral and administration costs out of the money of the estate. Their job is to apportion the estate as set out in the will. They should be kept informed of the location of all our assets. They need a financial understanding, an ability with paperwork and an attention to detail.

Do not name your spouse as sole executor because if both of you die together, then there is no living executor.

If you appoint a solicitor or a bank, be aware of the length of time it could take for your wishes to be finally realised. Waiting for probate to be finalised can be a frustrating process. It will also incur fees which mount over time.

As we prepare a list of our beneficiaries, we could include:

- A best friend;

- The child of a beloved relation;

- Grandchildren, who, without a specific clause in your will, are unlikely to receive anything;

- A trust fund: to encourage new writing, engineering, space travel – anything we have always loved and want to support;

- Decide who will administer the trust fund;

- Leaving a legacy to one or more charities of our choice.

You may have given generously all your life, and want to continue beyond your lifetime. Perhaps you already support charitable causes and want to make your giving continue.

You might want to leave an amount for others to distribute when you're gone. This is a Planned Giving Programme and there are many kinds of planned gifts. This is an arena where we need expert help. I offer a suggestion as to where you might start in looking for information.

Stewardship[80] is a well-established Christian charity with experience since 1906 in enabling generosity. It is designed for the things we want to set up without getting embroiled, as they say, in 'the fiddly bits'.

Using an initiative like Stewardship could well help us with long-term generosity without added complication to our loved ones.

Thinking about and putting things in place for long-term generosity could be fun.

Where to keep our will

Once made, our will should be kept in a safe place, without any other documents attached, where it can be found. It must be found to enable probate. Do make sure it can be found easily in the event of death.

- At home;

- A solicitor;

---

[80] www.stewardship.org.uk.

- A bank;

- Online;

- An executor.

Think carefully about using a bank safety deposit box because the bank cannot open it until the executor gets probate (permission from the court to administer our affairs). Probate cannot be granted without the will! This cannot be rectified if we are dead.

Rules of intestacy

Dying without drawing up a will means we die 'intestate'. If that happens then there are rules called 'Rules of Intestacy'.[81] These rules dictate how our under-age children, money, property or possessions will be allocated. Decisions could be taken that we would not want.

1. Unmarried partners who have not registered a civil partnership *cannot* inherit from each other without a will. This means the remaining partner could incur serious financial problems or lose their home.

2. There are two ways for couples to own their home. A beneficial joint-tenancy and tenancy-in-common. With the first, the surviving partner will automatically inherit the other partner's share of the property. It would not be automatic with the second.

---

[81] Intestacy, www.gov.uk; www.citizensadvice.org.uk.

3. Adopted children (including stepchildren adopted by their step-parent) have rights to inherit. Otherwise the child must be biological to inherit.

4. Children will inherit the whole estate from an intestate person if there is no surviving married or civil partner. If there are two or more it will be divided between them. If there is a surviving partner, they will only inherit if the estate is worth more than a certain amount. Check the website www.gov.uk for details.

5. Failure to make provision for under-age children should both parents die means bereft, grieving children may be cared for by relatives neither they nor their parents would wish. Therefore it is crucial to appoint a guardian for children in case they are orphaned before reaching the age of eighteen.

6. Make financial arrangements for the guardian for the considerable expenses. One way is to set up a Trust. Get advice.

7. Save money. A will could reduce the amount of tax payable.

8. Look after your business. If you are a sole director of a small business, your business could collapse if there are no executors authorised to make payments of bills and wages.

9. Close relatives may fail to inherit anything.

What you may not know about wills

1. Executors cannot pay out any bequests until all debts are discharged. This includes a mortgage and credit card bills.

2. Any live contract may be forced to finalise. For example, buying a house; the estate may have to complete the transaction.

3. Family cannot automatically be cut out of a will as they can legally challenge any will that deprives them of their perceived entitlement. To avoid costly and debilitating legal challenges which will only diminish the estate, discussion with the family is vital.

4. Electronic purchases do not belong to us. Many of us have built up huge libraries of music, films and books stored on our electronic devices. These cannot be passed on to the estate. Make sure someone, somewhere, holds the passwords or your collection will cease to exist once you do. Technically we have only purchased a licence to listen, to watch or to read.

5. Don't assume family can take care of your estate without a will. They will only be able to make decisions as the law dictates. Money and grief can destroy even the closest families.

Don't forget

1. Pet care. Make provision for all your pets.

2. Why not include funeral plans in the will? Only 30 per cent of us say we have talked about our funeral wishes.[82] Even fewer will actually have made a plan.

3. Make sure it is clear where your will is lodged. If online, somebody needs to know where and the relevant passwords, although a hard copy should be signed and kept safe.

4. Why not register as an organ donor? Less than a third (28 per cent) have registered despite the fact more than 1,000 people on the transplant waiting list die each year (NHS Blood and Transplant figures[83]). There is the opportunity to save other lives.

5. Don't forget to update your will! Circumstances change, relationships change. It is recommended this is done every five years.

6. If you have remarried, do ring-fence the share of the estate belonging to you. When we die that share will ultimately pass to our children after our partner's death, regardless of any remarriage of our partner. Or ring-fence a share for your children to receive immediately on your death. Otherwise your children may receive nothing and they may have no legal challenge available to them. On your death your spouse is entitled to dispose of assets as they wish without legal obligation to pass on any wealth to your children unless you have made it legally binding.

---

[82] ComRes interview. See note 23
[83] NHS Blood and Transplant (GB), www.organdonation.nhs.uk.

The above advice applies to England and can vary according to where we live in the UK. There are excellent websites[84] explaining the full rules of intestacy and the making of wills. Always check for the latest updates if you do not use a solicitor.

Replacing your will

If the original will is to be replaced by another then it must be clearly stated that the current document replaces all previous versions.

All previous versions should be destroyed.

Adding a codicil, something extra we have thought of, simply needs witnessing correctly and adding to the will.

A thought

A considerable amount of money needs to be accessible for expenses in the aftermath of a death. Monies from the estate are not made available until after probate and are dependent upon the executor/s.

My mother named one of my sisters as executor and cleverly added my sister's name on to her current account. It became their joint account. We found the access to money so helpful before probate came through as there were considerable expenses.

- Why not open a joint current account with one of your executors?

---

[84] www.citizensadvice.org.uk; www.gov.uk.

- Make your current account a joint account with a beneficiary?

Thoughtful provision means access to funds from the estate can be legal and immediate.

Deed of Variance

A person's will can be changed after their death, provided any beneficiaries left worse off by the changes agree. Any changes to the will must be completed within two years of death.[85] The Deed enables beneficiaries of the deceased's estate to alter the distribution of the estate. A bequest can also be relinquished.[86]

The fit and healthy father of a friend died unexpectedly. The expectation his wife would die before him was reflected in the will. Effectively his wife was disinherited by his death which would not have been her husband's intention. Their four adult children agreed and changed the will in order that their mother could access the funds she required.

The Deed of Variance for Inheritance Tax Planning is possibly subject to a government review at the time of writing.[87]

---

[85] 'Change a will after a death, www.gov.uk.
[86] 'Deed of Variation for changing a will', www.inbrief.co.uk.
[87] What is a Deed of Variation?', www.thorntons-law.co.uk.

Emotional will

An emotional will is a relatively new development and is an opportunity to leave more than your material goods.

You can leave your thoughts, your values, your lessons in life, special individual possessions to specific loved ones. You can ensure the stories attached to what you give, live on.

One of the things I did, as my husband and I have collected a few paintings/prints over the years, was to write a note on the back of each one - where we purchased it and why. Or, if a gift, who gave it to us.

One particular picture I love is from South Africa – a naïve picture composed entirely of beads, depicting a tree and an animal made by a woman who is part of a ladies' cooperative in that country. These ladies create the most astonishing beaded pictures. Their triumph, in my view, was a picture of a black Christ on a cross. The size was huge – metres wide and metres high – beautiful and moving. An exceptional altar piece in the right space. They came together as a group, along with their children, because they were HIV-positive.

The lady who made mine was so distraught at the news she was HIV-positive that she wanted to die and threw boiling oil over herself. Fortunately she didn't succeed. In her great distress she found community, companionship and purpose among the cooperative. I want her story to live on in my family.

Our family stories are important, I think. There are many in our family which are often recounted to the enjoyment of us all. It is part of our children's heritage. They value them. They love the photographs. On occasion the photos will be pulled off the shelves, or brought up on a screen, and shared memories recounted. I trust these will then be passed on to grandchildren.

I walk my family around our house pointing out their great-grandfather's roll-top desk, great-grandmother's display cabinet and blanket box, my father's 'gentleman's wardrobe'. The sticking point at the moment is the Clifford Family Bible. Both my children want that Bible.

We talk about these things. I think it is healthy. My death and the death of their father is as inevitable as theirs.

Here is my compilation of a few suggestions for an emotional will. What you might want to leave to someone specific.

- This is my favourite recipe because …

- This is my favourite book/film/poem/piece of music …

- I want you to keep the first record I ever bought because …

- This is my oldest piece of jewellery; it belonged to … I wore it …

- These cufflinks originally belonged to …

- This is the story of how your mum and dad met …

- This is the best present my husband/wife/partner ever gave me …

- One of my most important lessons in life is …

- This painting is important because …

- This piece of furniture was used by …

- Thank you so much for …
- A letter to particular family members. expressing your love for them; outlining a lovely memory …
- A letter of apology …
- This is my best memory …
- When you were born …
- Your friendship over the years has meant …

What might your own list contain?

An emotional will is a wonderful opportunity to reflect and be grateful.

Permissions

The question of giving permission and rights to the people we trust cannot be overemphasised. This must be done while we are of sound mind. I recognise this is difficult when we are feeling fit, mentally alert and physically able.

This is about taking control rather than relinquishing it.

It doesn't mean we are about to disintegrate.

Let me recount my friend Jill's story. I know many will empathise.

Jill is a former solicitor. She and her siblings have two parents in their nineties. While the parents are living alone together in their home, there are health difficulties at different times. They live a lengthy car journey away from their nearest health centre.

If Jill is to communicate with the health centre regarding either parent, even as a member of the nuclear family, a written consent document must be in place. The document must be signed by the parent and a witness. The witness must have known both the patient and the family member for a minimum of two years. Should the husband and wife each wish to be given information concerning the other, they too must have a signed document. Jill's parents have been married for sixty-eight years. Whereas doctors can show some discretion in disseminating information, receptionists and others in a health centre cannot. Permission must be evident on the screen that the person calling is authorised to speak and receive information regarding the named person of their enquiry.

The health centre Jill is dealing with doesn't send these permission forms out by post. Her parents are too elderly to jump into a car, park, collect the forms and return home. The forms can be downloaded but the couple do not have a computer and do not own a printer.

This is enormous hassle in a stressful and pressured time. Jill does not live in the same area. She visits when she can. Time is precious and when she is with them she wants to communicate with the surrounding professionals without delay.

If she goes to the health centre with them, then she is allowed entrance to the doctor's room as an escort. She will not be permitted to speak during the consultation. She may not answer on their behalf or contribute unless the doctor present bends the rules. The rules are designed to protect against manipulation or bullying. It does not lessen Jill's frustration.

Finally the appropriate forms are completed and signed. How much easier if consent had been given earlier by her parents, ready for just such an occasion.

Both her parents have cash cards allowing them to withdraw money. Her mother forgot the PIN number and needed a new one. Jill had to speak for her mother because she is deaf on the phone. It went backwards and forwards for three-quarters of an hour, with Jill identifying her mother and then asking her mother the security questions, the answers to none of which her mother could remember. Communication broke down.

They were instructed to visit a local branch. Her mother was immobile. There was no parking outside the branch. It was impossible.

After that the family kept a file so they could have the questions and answers accessible because a ninety-plus person may not recall them.

All problems are solvable but the price is stress and anxiety. It is important to think things through in advance.

Health centres and other institutional bodies

Consider the following:

- Make sure a written consent is signed and witnessed if you wish to contribute in a full consultation on the health of anyone in your family, including your spouse. If not, you may be present but unable to ask or say anything.

- Forms are obtainable from the relevant centres.

- Being part of the nuclear family does not give automatic permission.

There are two important ways to retain our health choices:

- A Lasting Power of Attorney (LPA) – this incurs costs.
- An Advance Decision (Living Will) – this is free.

As always, there are pros and cons. The final document drawn up overrides the former.

The LPA is only valid once correctly witnessed and registered with the Office of the Public Guardian. This can take up to eight weeks.

The Advance Decision comes into effect as soon as it is correctly signed and witnessed.

You can have both an Advance Decision and an LPA in place.

Lasting Power of Attorney[88]

If you are like me, then I worry about the process of dying even more than my actual death. It would have been so much easier for myself and my sisters if our mother had

---

[88] *Compassion in Dying*, www.compassionindying.org.uk. The site includes downloadable forms.
NHS Choices, 'End of life care; Advanced decision (living will)', www.nhs.uk.
'A Guide to Making Your Lasting Power of Attorney', www.lastingpowerofattorney.service.gov.uk.

written a Lasting Power of Attorney or made an Advance Decision.

Why?

There is a General Power of Attorney (POA). This General POA allows you to give legal permission to someone else to take decisions and sign documents on your behalf while you still have mental capacity.

- You are in hospital and you need someone else to organise your money for a time.

- If you want to give someone the power to act as if they were you on a short term basis only.

- If you have 'mental capacity' to understand fully what you are signing.

- Only applicable if you live in England or Wales.

- This is only used for financial matters.

- A General POA becomes effective immediately. It remains in place until the donor cancels it.

- If the donor becomes mentally incapable the POA is revoked.

- A General POA does not allow any restrictions on the attorney's powers. This differs from an LPA.

You must absolutely trust the person or persons you appoint in your General Power of Attorney.

A Lasting Power of Attorney (LPA)[89]

This gives authority to one or more named persons should you lose mental capacity[90] and are unable to make your own decisions. If you regain your mental capacity, for example, after an accident where you are unconscious, you may then take the appropriate steps to revoke your LPA.

The Mental Capacity Act allows for the fact that people may lack capacity to make some decisions for themselves, but will have capacity to make other decisions. For example, they can make small, everyday decisions, but cannot make more complex ones. It allows that capacity changes according to illness or condition, ie you recover consciousness and function fully. The aim of the Act is to make sure people are given the right help and support to make their own decisions. It applies only in England and Wales.

Always discuss your decisions thoroughly with trustworthy people in order that the right safeguards are put in place for you.

1.   A Lasting Power of Attorney (LPA) can be awarded both for financial matters and for personal welfare and health. You can choose to have an LPA for personal welfare and health alone.

---

[89] *The Law Society*, www.lawsociety.org.uk.
[90] 'A person who lacks capacity to make a particular decision or take a particular action for themselves at the time the decision or action needs to be taken.' (The Mental Capacity Act 2005 Code of Practice, www.gov.uk.)

2. An LPA allows you to place power for your well-being into other hands. When you cannot function, those you have named can become your decision-makers. This includes:

    -   Where the donor should live;

    -   Day-to-day care;

    -   Whether to give or refuse consent to medical treatment.

3. You can appoint different people _– one for your financial affairs; one for your personal health and welfare.

4. An LPA can be set up for anyone aged eighteen or older. The person (the donor) needs to have the mental capacity to make a future decision that the person or persons they name will have the power to decide treatment and care should they, the donor, lose capacity.

    For example: without a legal document such as an LPA or an Advance Decision, if something medically traumatic happens and I am completely incapacitated, my husband cannot legally be the overriding voice in my care. The medical profession become that authority.

5. The LPA must state whether your attorney has the power to decide about life-sustaining treatment. If they do not have that power, then all decisions about life-sustaining treatment are taken by the healthcare

team (unless an Advance Decision has been drawn up after the LPA).

6.   An LPA once registered is entered on a register at the Office of the Public Guardian (OPG) accessible to healthcare professionals. If doctors need to find out the legality of someone claiming to be your attorney without the requisite paperwork, then they must apply to the OPG directly. The search would generally take seven working days. This is not true of an Advance Decision.

7.   You can appoint several attorneys on the LPA. This gives decision-making to the person or persons named. They will, if necessary, decide about the welfare of the donor. This could include where you will live and all aspects of your health and welfare. You could appoint your spouse and your adult children. Should a decision be required, you could decide only two of those named need to be present.

8.   The LPA will only be effective once the person has lost the capacity to make their own decisions. For information and pack contact gov.uk[91] or the Office of the Public Guardian (OPG[92]).

9.   If a decision must be taken in a scenario unspecified by the Advance Decision, then our attorney will act on

---

[91] www.gov.uk. Search: Power of attorney. *Power of Attorney Age UK*, www.ageuk.org.uk.

[92] Office of the Public Guardian (OPG) where the Power of Attorney is registered: www.gov.uk. Search: Office of the Public Guardian.

our behalf. Although if the situation is unspecified in either document, it could revert back to the medical profession.

10. Each attorney should have a copy in safe-keeping of your LPA.

11. Revoking your LPA can be done as long as you have the mental capacity to understand what you are doing. My question: who would decide my mental capacity? I rang the Office of the Public Guardian, and mental capacity would generally be decided by interview and there are various examples of capacity assessments available online. It could be done by a GP.

12. Dissolution or annulment of a marriage or civil partnership will automatically revoke the legality of your partner/spouse being your attorney.

13. *Lasting Power of Attorney does not come into force until you need it*, even once you have registered your LPA. It is not legal unless registered with the Office of the Public Guardian.

14. Should the attorneys be deemed not to be acting in your best interests at all times, then appeal, on your behalf, can be made to the Public Guardian and the Court of Protection.

15. There is always a risk of abuse of an LPA, therefore the appointment of an attorney or attorneys should be done with the utmost care. It may well be prudent not to have a single attorney.

16. A valid LPA must include a certificate completed by an independent third party.

How do we set it up?

1. Online forms[93] will lead you through the process. They can be filled in online, or downloaded, printed and completed.

2. Fees can be processed online.

3. The completed LPA forms must be printed and signed by all relevant parties in the presence of a witness who has known you for two or more years. This witness is the Certificate Provider who supplies a legal certificate. They will certify when the form was signed, that you:

    *   understood the purpose and scope of the authority being granted;

    *   were not being unduly pressured;

    *   were not affected by anything which could invalidate the document.

4. If more than one are named attorneys in the LPA, then you may specify whether they can make decisions jointly and are bound to come to agreement together, or whether severally ie one could made a decision. You can decide how many need to agree to make a decision.

5. Other decisions could be individual, by a named person.

6. The LPA must be printed, (the deed) signed, and sent to the Office of the Public Guardian (OPG) for

---

[93] www.gov.uk; www.nhs.uk.

registration in order for it to come into force when needed.

7. There are various provisos to attorney power. It is advisable to study this in depth.

8. The Lasting Power of Attorney can be cancelled at any time by the donor, even if registered. However, the donor must have the mental capacity to make that decision. They must inform their attorneys and the OPG for the removal of the LPA from the register.

Why might we revoke an LPA?

- Things change in life.

- An attorney may die.

- A marriage or civil partnership may end and the donor might not wish the attorney to remain the same.

If you write a Lasting Power of Attorney, remember to keep it up to date.

Ending a Lasting Power of Attorney[94]

1. You need to make a written statement called a 'deed of revocation'. This must be witnessed. The wording for the 'deed' is on the gov.uk website (see below).

2. This must be sent to the Office of the Public Guardian.

3. The attorney(s) must be informed.

---

[94] www.gov.uk. Search: Power of Attorney.

Evoking the Lasting Power of Attorney

1. Once evoked, the LPA will remain in place.

2. If you regain your mental capacity – eg, recover from a traumatic illness – and wish to make your own decisions regarding your health and welfare, then you must evidence this through an appropriate professional, such as a GP or social worker.

3. The Office of the Public Guardian must be informed as well as your attorney(s).[95]

4. You do not need to revoke your LPA. It may remain in place.

All this information should be checked as details change regularly.

End-of-life care

What do you want?

You need to think about treatment in your end-of-life care, when you cannot make important decisions.

We all make different choices, and it is important to choose. Our country has a great NHS, with doctors and nurses who work tirelessly to save lives, but their mandate is to keep people alive. We need to ask ourselves the hard questions.

•   Do you wish to be kept alive at any cost?

---

[95] Information from Office of Public Guardian.

- Is there a point of incapacity you could not bear? For example: my mother did not want to be kept alive on a ventilator.

Our Attorney or Advance Decision nominee/s has the power to agree to any medical treatment and the authority to stop healthcare treatment in line with our wishes.

As God-lovers we have a different world view. Death is not the worst thing that will happen to us.

Care homes and visiting

As an aside, Helen Calder, a friend who worked for years at the Evangelical Alliance and is now freelance, put together some helpful lists. As a single woman, she found herself responsible after the deaths of several relatives. I thought these lists would be useful, and have included them as Appendices 1, 2 and 3.

Why is organising end-of-life care important?

The statistics (British Social Attitudes 30[96]) show that only 5 per cent of us have set out how we would want to be cared for at the end of our lives. Only 1 per cent[97] have initiated a conversation with their GP about their end-of-life wishes. Forty-five per cent agree that talking or thinking about end of life planning makes death feel closer. Forty-five per cent say they are too scared to talk about it.[98]

---

[96] British Social Attitudes Survey, www.bsa.natcen.ac.uk; Attitudes to Death, Dying and Bereavement pdf.

[97] ComRes interview. See note 23.

[98] ComRes interview. See note 23.

A huge 67 per cent of us want to be able to die at home. (The End of Life Care Strategy[99] aims to support more people to die in their preferred place.)

Hospices and palliative or support care units are the second most common preference. For most of us the important thing is to be pain-free for a 'good death'.[100]

At the beginning of the twentieth century it was common for people to die at home. Today, hospital remains the most common place of death.

The presence of a family or informal carer is a key to achieving a home death with effective and sustained carer support, especially during longer illnesses. Perhaps we need more communication at an earlier stage with the palliative/support care experts available to us so we can really understand all that can be done at home.

Quality information diminishes fear and distress.

Advance Decision (Living Will)

This is a way to make known the wishes, values and preferences to be addressed when you may be unable to speak for yourself or lose mental capacity. Compassion in Dying[101] have a superb Advance Decision Pack which allows you to make decisions about your care, but also includes an Advance Directive to Refuse Treatment

---

[99] 'End of Life Care Strategy', Department of Health (2008), www.gov.uk.

[100] ComRes interview. See note 23.

[101] Compassion in Dying, www.compassionindying.org.uk, Advance Decision Pack; Age UK, http://www.ageuk.org.uk, free downloadable information leaflets.

(ADRT). Once signed it is a legal document and anyone responsible for your care must follow your instructions.

I found it challenging to fill in the form. Thinking about my preferences in the light of any incapacity I might suffer was definitely emotionally uncomfortable. However, it left me feeling:

1. My family were now empowered in decision-making regarding my care;

2. I was empowered to die with dignity.

Reasons to make it

1. Peace of mind; your wishes will be paramount when, for whatever reason, you cannot make a decision about your medical care.

2. As with a will regarding your possessions, this is to make decisions about your future care.

3. To release family members from burden and distress, unsure about decisions they must take on your behalf. You may not be comfortable to leave medical professionals to decide your 'best interests'.

4. To allow you to express any strong wishes you have concerning your medical care, for example, in the event of a catastrophic occurrence that leaves you in a persistent vegetative state.

What could I include?

*   Do you want to be told you are dying?

*   Who do you name to speak for you?

- Where would you like to die?

- You may want to refuse treatment in some circumstances, but not all.

- You might not want CPR (an emergency treatment to restart the heart and breathing which includes inserting a tube into the windpipe to inflate the lungs).

- You might not want defibrillation (the use of electric shocks to restart and correct the heart's rhythm).

- The long-term or lifelong use of a ventilator to help you breathe if you cannot do it on our own.

You can choose to refuse any treatment, including life-sustaining treatment, while relying on the healthcare team to keep you comfortable and pain-free.

You need to be specific so your wishes are not open to interpretation. An example of possible confusion: stating you want to refuse life-sustaining treatment if your 'suffering becomes unbearable'. The point at which your suffering becomes 'unbearable' could be perceived differently by different people. It could mean your instruction is not followed because your doctor does not know exactly when to apply it.

If you had written in your Advance Decision that you only wanted to refuse life-sustaining treatment if you were in a persistent vegetative state, you might still be given treatment under other circumstances.

What treatment you want to refuse and the situations in which you want to refuse it need to be crystal clear. All this you can outline and the forms on the website come with excellent Guidance Notes to help you think clearly.

An Advance Decision cannot be used to refuse treatment if you still have the capacity to make the decision yourself.

You cannot use an Advance Decision to:

- ask for an assisted death, because assisted dying is against the law in the UK;

- refuse food and drink by mouth or basic care that attends to your comfort, and/or personal hygiene, because these are basic human rights. However, you can refuse food and water intravenously as this is termed 'medical treatment';

- nominate someone else to decide about treatment on your behalf. You can only do this through the attorney/s you have nominated in a Lasting Power of Attorney;

- demand certain treatments. Our treatment is the doctors' decision. We may only decide which treatment we may or may not want.

It is legally binding in England and Wales (check for the rest of the UK). If ignored, a doctor could face criminal prosecution or civil liability.

If you acquire a life-threatening illness, you can update the Advance Decision to account for a more specific illness as clarity comes as to what you do and do not want. The form must be witnessed and dated on completion and for every update. No solicitor is required. It is a legal document.

It is important to communicate with those you love about your decisions. Why not include them in the decision-making process? It is helpful to talk it through with others and/or your GP for insight into what treatments to include/exclude. The GP could be a signatory, and vouch for your 'capacity' (ie you had full mental capacity when writing your Advance Decision).

After legalising your Advance Decision through witnesses, you might then decide to create a Lasting Power of Attorney. This LPA will then take precedence over your Advance Decision. An LPA will allow your attorney/s to make decisions on your behalf. However, if you then update your Advance Decision and sign and date it, this will again take precedence. This was a question I put to 'Compassion in Dying', who assured me this would be the case.

Advance Decisions (AD) come into effect as soon as the document has been signed and witnessed correctly. An LPA is only valid once registered with the Office of the Public Guardian, which can take up to eight weeks. Unlike the LPA the AD is free, and only needs one witness.

Advance Decisions only apply to the specific treatments and circumstances you write about in the document. Anything outside will not be included. However, your attorney can make any decision about our health and welfare on our behalf, interpreting our wishes, whether or not we designated our specific situation at the time of writing.

How will people know?

Loved ones and the healthcare professionals need to be aware we have an Advance Decision. Here are some suggestions:

- our GP (ask him to add notice of an AD to our electronic Summary Care Record);

- our loved ones;

- executor/s of our will;

- any person regularly involved in our care;

- a 'Notice of Advance Decision' card (which comes with Compassion in Dying's Advance Decision pack);

- our attorney;

- keep a copy ourselves;

- join MedicAlert for an annual fee who will provide us with jewellery to wear with important details engraved on the back and will also store an electronic copy of our AD.

Review and update regularly

If your health changes or you are going into hospital for any reason, you should review and update your Advance Decision. Compassion for Dying strongly recommend the review occurs every two years, even with stable health.

An Advance Decision that is regularly reviewed is more likely to be 'valid' and 'applicable' to the current circumstances, and so healthcare professionals can be more confident that they are acting in your 'best interests'.

- New and improved medical treatments may have become available.

- Your personal circumstances may have changed.

Its validity may be questioned if it has not been reviewed for years.

How to cancel an Advance Decision

This can be done any time, as long as you retain the capacity to do so. There is no formal process to follow. It can be done in writing or verbally and the original document can be destroyed. All who knew of the Advance Decision should be informed. Putting it in writing avoids uncertainty.

This information has been compiled from the following websites in 2017:

www.dyingmatters.org
www.compassionindying.org.uk
www.ageuk.org.uk
www.macmillan.org.uk
www.nhs.uk
www.alzheimers.org.uk

All documents and guides can be downloaded from www.compassionindying.org.uk.

The website www.healthtalk.org has videos and written interviews of people talking about Advance Decision to refuse treatment.

Burials and funerals

Burial choices

During the time I spent with Mary, my lovely ninety year old Sri Lankan lady, she was keen to organise her funeral. She has some health difficulties. She is not afraid of death. Talking with her was an inspiration.

I realised I didn't know much about her life. 'Old people' are often put in a category of being 'old'. Not seen as 'people', they become an embodiment of something we want to avoid. If we take time to talk with them, we can learn about the world through their experiences – the pain and pleasure, failures and successes. Many deserve honour for their contribution to our society.

Mary arrived in the UK just after she had married at forty-one. I laughed when she told me she had lied about her age and told her husband she was thirty-five. I don't think he ever found out. She was a nurse and worked in London hospitals and prisons. She had a difficult relationship with her adopted daughter. Her husband died ten years ago. Our church became her family.

While she chose us, when she dies, to perform her funeral service, Mary's burial choice was to be sent back to Sri Lanka.

How much do funerals cost?

I watched this very helpful programme: ITV *Tonight*:[102] End of Life Survey (1,000 adults surveyed):

---

[102] *Tonight*, 'Funerals: a costly undertaking' (ITV, 4th November 2016).

- 78 per cent of adults have not done any research into funeral options.

- 53 per cent of adults have not communicated funeral wishes to their loved ones.

- 62 per cent of adults didn't know how much the average funeral cost.

- 44 per cent of adults didn't know how they would make up a shortfall in funeral costs with 30 per cent saying they would put the money on a credit card.

- 49 per cent of adults who had organised a funeral said that knowing the wishes of the deceased made it easier to organise and pay for the send-off.

- The average cost of a funeral is £3,675 (much more around London, I found).

- People were offered many unnecessary extras.

- Funerals will be the biggest credit card spend – 93,000 people in UK in 2016.

Interviewees in the programme made the point that often a death is sudden and unexpected. You are grieving. At a funeral director's, you are given a catalogue and then expected to go shopping for something you don't want. One woman said that is was an experience that was surreal. Her funeral bill came to £4,500 and at no point was she asked if she could afford it. The programme urged us to:

- Ask the price (first price for one client was £7,000 – he said he couldn't afford it).

- Then ask for the best price (revised price £2,200 for the same client).

- Walk away if it is too much – the cheapest (November 2016) is about £1,500.[103]

On the ITV *Tonight* programme, a daughter collected her mother in a coffin into their camper van. Drove round their usual haunts. Took her to the sea. Organised a plot. Dug a grave herself, and buried her. No cost apart from diesel for the van.

Things you might not know

- The law does not require the use of a funeral director or for a funeral service to be held.

- The person who engages an undertaker is responsible for paying the bill.

- You can be buried in a private or local authority cemetery, Church of England or other religious burial ground, nature reserve, or other land, provided the owner gives prior permission.[104]

- You can be buried at sea, but it is difficult to arrange and very expensive.

- You don't have to be buried or cremated, you can be preserved, although someone will have to take ownership of your body.

---

[103] From *The cost of dying*, www.sunlife.co.uk.
[104] See 'Planning a green funeral/burial'.

- You can give your body for medical research.

- If you ask someone to take possession of your body they will have a duty to dispose of it in a legal way.

- Any Christian denomination can conduct a funeral in a Church of England burial place.

- You can do anything you like at a funeral so long as it is within the law – and the regulations of the venue

- You have the right to have your body cared for at home and have a 'Do it Yourself'[105] funeral.

Direct cremation[106]

- A basic service.

- No choice over time or date. It can happen very quickly.

- No choice over which crematorium.

The funeral director simply collects the deceased, organises the paperwork, provides a basic coffin, books a convenient time and carries out the cremation.

A basic cremation should include:

- the funeral director's services;

- a coffin;

_____

[105] Charles Cowling, *The Good Funeral Guide* (London: Continuum, 2010).
[106] The only direct cremation specialist in the UK is www.simplicitycremations.co.uk.

- transfer of person from place of death;
- care of person prior to funeral (you can ask to see them before the funeral);
- a hearse for transport;
- all required arrangements and paperwork;
- check price of anything extra to this.

A direct cremation is a way of preparing a body for a funeral. The ashes are then available for a funeral, memorial, or Celebration of Life service.

A cremation is generally cheaper than a burial.

One man I met knew his atheist father would have hated any funeral or service. He made a cardboard coffin for him, hired a white van, went to the hospital and placed his father in the coffin. He drove with his friend to the crematorium and his father was cremated at the cheapest time of the day. He collected the ashes and scattered them. He truly believed this would honour his father's wishes. A solution not for the faint-hearted, I suggest.

If you are thinking of having no ceremony at all, then I add a note of caution. Funerals are more for the living than for the dead. For many, some sort of ceremony following the death of a loved one is an important part of the grieving process. You may think it is unnecessary, but having walked alongside someone whose mother wanted nothing at all, I realised how difficult that was for her four children. Our death is not so much about ourselves, it is more about those we leave. Let us strive to leave well.

Guidelines for a cremation or burial[107]

- Check to see if the deceased has paid into a funeral plan, a life insurance policy, or pension scheme for funeral costs.

- Do it the way you feel it should be done.

- Don't rush; the UK, unlike Holland, does not require the funeral to occur within one week. Some religions do require burial within twenty-four hours.

- Shop around – there is so much on offer and a lot of money can be saved. Ask for quotations on expenses. Are there extra charges for embalming, crematorium or cemetery fees, clergy? You don't have to have a body embalmed.

- Choose an undertaker if you wish, although that is not mandatory. An undertaker is an agent. They are employed to do what you wish.

- Use the internet; it has so much information.

Cremation?

- Cheaper, and you can keep the ashes. Also cheaper to scatter or place in a burial ground.

Burial?

- Don't assume it is easy to buy a burial plot. You usually are buying at least two at the same time (one coffin to be buried on top of another). They are not

---

[107] Cowling, *The Good Funeral Guide*, chapters 8 and 9.

necessarily available where you want. It might only be for a period of thirty years. Especially difficult in cities and certainly in London. I was shocked. A good reason to make a decision beforehand.

- Natural burial ground – natural and gradual, with room for artefacts to be buried with the person. More eco-friendly if body is not embalmed.

- You can buy the lease for between fifty and 100 years for the exclusive right to burial in a particular plot in a woodland burial. More space and you could buy several plots to include the family.

Burial at sea?

- Possible where there is no hazard to shipping.

- Need to obtain a free licence from DEFRA.[108]

Burial in your own garden?

- No official permission required, but DEFRA will want to be sure there is no contamination of water supplies.

- Advisable to record the burial on the deeds, which could lower the value of the house.

- If the house is sold, visiting rights may be withheld.

- The new owners could exhume the body.

---

[108] See *The Natural Death Handbook*, fifth edition, ed. Ru Callender (London: Strange Attractor, 2012). Available online from The Natural Death Centre, www.naturaldeath.org.uk and in selected bookshops.

Planning a green funeral/burial[109]

There are now hundreds of natural burial sites all around the UK (see Association of Natural Burial Grounds, ANBG). You may want as environmentally friendly burial as possible. There are now many different ways to do this. For example, you could opt to be buried with a tree that is part of a copse. It is in that copse that your friends and family could gather to remember you. These DIY funerals can be less expensive and more personal, intimate and supposedly environmentally friendly.[110]

Things to consider:

• The advantage of the ANBG is that they have a Code of Conduct.

• Not all coffins (for burial) are environmentally friendly.

• Embalming, which uses chemicals toxic to the environment, is unnecessary and generally unacceptable in natural burial grounds.

• Only single depth burials are used, as a shallow burial is the quickest way for the body to degrade naturally.

• Headstones or other memorialisation are not always allowed. Sometimes there is no tending of the grave. (A decision that needs careful consideration for the living.) Do check.

---

[109] Association of Natural Burial Grounds (ANBG), www.anbg.co.uk; www.naturaldeath.org.uk. *The Natural Death Handbook*.
[110] Cowling, *The Good Funeral Guide*, chapter 6.

Bethany Church,[111] Southall

Bethany Church is a Tamil-speaking Christian community in Southall. The leaders, Rev T. M. I. Sathiyaraj and his wife, Pastor Chrishanthy Sathiyaraj, have put a great deal of thought into burial plans.

Asian people, explains Chrishanthy, do not like to think about or discuss dying and death. They feel it is bad luck to talk about it. However, with great foresight, Chrishanthy arranged 100 plots in a nearby woodland burial site, buying them on a 100-year lease. She has called the area Bethany Woods. This is to create burial space for as many in the church as possible, so they may all be buried in the same area. She has plots for her entire family. Each grave allows for a small wooden memorial. Her forward thinking will mean a whole community will lie together. Whenever anyone visits, or a new person is buried, friends and family will be able to wander and remember loved ones together.

She has encouraged many in the church to sign up for it and they pay a small amount each month towards their plot. She recognised the cost to a church member to be sent back in a coffin to their country of origin would be prohibitive. This way a beautiful woodland setting is prepared for each one.

As pressure grows on city burial plots, it is a clever plan. Chrishanthy's enquiries revealed that in Southall most burial plots may only be leased initially for thirty years. In nearby Greenford, to buy a plot will cost upwards of £2,000. Cremation is, of course, cheaper, though over

---

[111] Bethany Church, www.bfminternational.org.

£1,000. My own enquiries revealed the same. Unplanned funerals with people who have limited finances can cause people to incur a crippling debt. I find the far-sightedness of Bethany Church refreshing and thought-provoking. I also am challenged by the notion of a church community who have lived and worked together being buried together.

I visited this woodland burial site and was captivated by the beauty of the area. There was also a lovely woodland hall available for a funeral and/or memorial service. The notion of going to look where you might want to be buried or have your ashes scattered, while initially unnerving, was in fact a hugely positive experience, one I want my husband to discover as well. My thoughts were not for myself, rather for those saying goodbye to me. It would ease a sad farewell to be in the midst of a stunning and life-affirming environment. I say again, our death is not only about us, but also about our loved ones.

Making your own funeral choice

- Some idea of your choice of funeral will be enormously helpful to your family.

- Regarding funeral directors, why not make a shortlist of up to six with names and phone numbers?

- Have a list of questions for your family to ask in order to choose the right director. I am assuming most of us will not want to impose a do-it-yourself funeral on loved ones unless you are part of an active community.

- *The Good Funeral Guide*[112] has an excellent list of questions in chapter 38 (p. 158) to help think this through.

- The cost of funerals varies enormously. It is worth checking on the Financial Conduct Authority site, www.fca.org.uk, regarding 'funeral services' or 'funeral plans', as it will list unauthorised bodies.

- It might be possible to get a grant from the Social Fund[113] to help towards funeral costs.

Seeing your dead loved one

It is worth taking a moment to think about whether you wish to see your loved one again once they have died, whatever the circumstances. The undertaker/hospital can arrange it. It is possible to have the body returned home to do this.

- It might help accept their death and let them go.

- You might have something you wish to say.

- It can be a reality check that your world has changed.

- It may provide a peaceful last moment, perhaps in contrast to their death.

---

[112] Cowling, *The Good Funeral Guide*.

[113] The Social Fund, www.citizensadvice.org.uk. The Social Fund, technical guidance – publications www.gov.uk/government/publications/the-social-fund-technical-guidance.

Organising the Ceremony/Celebration of Life service

Many now choose to have a Celebration of Life service. Often close family only are then present at the burial site or the crematorium.

It is a good idea to talk with those with experience in this area. If you are near the end of your life, perhaps ask the person you choose to conduct your ceremony to help you to design it.

Things to think about

- What will be the tone of the event? Solemn, celebratory, reflective, or a mix of different moods?

- How do you want people to feel when the service has finished?

- Where will the service take place?
  - a church – will the coffin be present?
  - a room hired for the event – will the coffin be present?
  - the crematorium;
  - the graveyard;
  - a natural burial site.

- Will you have two events – the burial, and the ceremony?

- What do you want the celebration/service to achieve?

- Whom would you like to participate?

- Collect songs, hymns, poems, readings that you like.

- Decide how you want the guests to be refreshed afterwards.

- Include family and friends in your decisions – they will love to know that they are participating in something that you have been so active in organising.

An interesting note is that the Rev Billy Graham, a preacher all his life, has already recorded his final sermon which will be shown at his funeral/celebration of his life. Not for everyone, but the man dying as he had lived.

The pre-ceremony

- Create a memory board or table. This could be not only photographs, but also objects of importance. Pictures drawn/painted, much-loved books.

- Prepare a short account of your life for the order of service – what would you like people to know about you?

- Collect photographs and mementos of your life to display.

- A Book of Remembrance for all those present to write in.

The ceremony

This is an opportunity for you to choose your favourite music, readings, poems, thoughts and gather photos that you feel will express your life; also to choose the people you would like to contribute. You could even write or record something to be spoken or played at the ceremony.

Pictures of your life could be shown on a loop as people gather.

Order of Service

1. Leader: The beginning – welcome and/or entry of coffin – music. At a crematorium, of course, the coffin will be in full sight of those gathered.

2. Speaker 1: The loved one – life story highlights.

3. Music/song – either the whole gathering or a favourite song played or sung live.

4. Speaker 2: Memories and/or a short reading.

5. Music/song – either the whole gathering or a favourite song played or sung live.

6. Speaker 3: Memories and/or a short reading/poem.

7. Music/song – either the whole gathering or a favourite song played or sung live.

8. Speaker 4: Reflection/talk and prayer.

9. Leader: Committal and prayers.

10. Music/song – either the whole gathering or a favourite song played or sung live.

11. Leader: Dismiss the gathering and invite those present to refreshment.

The Church of England does this so well. If you want a set service, I recommend their website: www.churchofengland.org. They split the outline order into six points:

- The Gathering;

- Readings and sermon;

- Prayers;

- Commendation and farewell;

- The Committal;

- The Dismissal;

The post-ceremony

You have an opportunity to think about how you would like those gathered at the ceremony to be hosted and refreshed. What tone would you like to set?

> How people die remains in the memory of those who live on.
> *Dame Cicely Saunders*[114]

(See Appendix 1 for a comprehensive list of what needs to be done after a loved one has died.)

---

[114] Dame Cicely Saunders, founder of the modern hospice movement.

Last Rites

Well Marianne it's come to this time when we are really
so old and our bodies are falling apart and I think I will
follow you very soon.
Know that I am so close behind you that if you stretch out
your hand, I think you can reach mine. And you know
that I've always loved you for your beauty and your
wisdom, but I don't need to say anything more about that
because you know all about that. But now, I just want to
wish you a very good journey. Goodbye old friend.
Endless love, see you down the road.
Leonard Cohen, 2016[115]

Leonard Cohen's now famous letter was written when he
heard of the imminent death of his muse and lover,
Marianne Ihlen. It was a beautiful gift to a woman he loved
very much. She died a few days after receiving it. He knew
that his own death was looming and he said goodbye
elegantly and eloquently.

Last words are not always so. Jesus was deeply afraid.

'My soul is overwhelmed with sorrow to the point
of death. Stay here and keep watch with me.' Going
a little farther, he fell with his face to the ground and
prayed, 'My Father, if it is possible, may this cup be
taken from me. Yet not as I will, but as you will.'
Matthew 26:38–39

---

[115] CBC Radio, *As It Happens*, 3rd August 2016,
www.cbc.ca/radio/asithappens. Permission given to use from
the show although they do not own copyright of the quotation.
Every effort has been made to locate the copyright holder.

Listening to a BBC radio programme and the stories of those who sat with their dying loved ones, it struck me how many had little idea what to expect. Our learning about such events is often based on the media and far from reality.

In media dying, the dear one lies hovering between life and death. Precious last words are spoken. Often these are words of comfort. A mother expressing her love for her child; another asks for forgiveness in their dying moments. A secret comes to light and long-held puzzlements fall into place. The scriptwriter/author gives voice to things unspoken. The final moment draws a line of closure. This isn't how it happens.

It becomes even more important that you have given yourself the opportunity to say goodbye while you have mental capacity.

A person suffering from dementia will be unable to bring any conclusion. Often they slip into unconsciousness and families wait in limbo for the moment of death.

Some people do not want to die with their loved ones present. In a last act of self-determination they choose to die when the room is empty. Do not feel guilty if that happened to you.

Others wait until the loved one arrives. This happened with the mother of my friend. As soon as my friend walked into the room and took her hand, her mother died. I watched it happen.

One lady on a BBC radio programme spoke of disappointment when her mother died. She felt inadequate, as if things remained unfinished. It still haunts her several times a day. Her mother has been dead six years.

None of us want to leave our loved ones in a daily state of 'unfinished business' or anxiety. Let's think how to bring closure so those we leave can release us and continue with their lives.

It is crucial that we, as loved ones, say our goodbyes to the person dying. It will be difficult and emotional, and I am sure we will falter. We are learners. I cannot emphasise how good and releasing it is to speak and let that person go. It might be months before they actually die, but saying goodbye will bring release not only for you but also for them. You give them permission to leave.

My grandmother died when she was 101. I remember we gathered regularly as a family to celebrate 'big' birthdays. As a child I had stayed with her on occasion by myself. She was fearsome but good-hearted and kind to me.

When I was twelve, Granny bought me a dress with green circles on it which I loved. At her ninetieth birthday celebration I made a beeline for her. She was my father's mother. She and I had spoken little for decades, as my parents had divorced. I sat next to her and thanked her profusely for buying me that dress. It was very important to me that she knew.

It wasn't the last time I saw her but, however inexplicable, I remain so pleased I said that. As I write this it still brings a lump to my throat. I don't think she remembered buying the dress. But I did it for me, not only for her. It was my way of saying goodbye.

Who are you?

What would you like your family/carers to know?[116]

- Shower or bath?

- Michael Bublé, Brahms, The Beatles or Bruno Mars? Own home or care home or hospital? If away from home, find a way to take home with you – use photos, diaries, laptop or tablet. It allows carers to talk to you about your life.

- Advance Decision? Have you filled in the form? Have you had it witnessed? As soon as it is witnessed, it becomes legal.

- Lasting Power of Attorney – can your loved ones make the decisions you want?

- What are your preferred priorities for Advanced Care Planning?[117]

Without planning, decisions will be taken out of your hands. It is likely events will mean hospital admission under the care and decisions of doctors. This could be what you want. You have a choice.

You can't plan if you don't talk.

You can't make life easier for family and friends if you don't talk.

---

[116] See Appendix 2: 'Choosing a care home or nursing home'.
[117] *Thinking and Planning Ahead: Resource List*,
www.dyingmatters.org.
Advance Care Planning, www.ncpc.org.uk.

There will be others in the same position as you. Can you find a group where you can talk?

Hopefully this book will help you chart a course that brings peace of mind because you have been involved in choosing everything you wish.

Age UK produces LifeBook,[118] a free, easy way – downloadable (or have it posted to you) – to record important and useful information about your life.

Hospice care[119]

While there are hospices where people with less than six months to live can take up residence and be cared for, hospice care is a style of care. It places a high value on dignity, respect and patient wishes.

They aim to provide holistic care, ie for medical, emotional, social, practical, psychological and spiritual needs. They would also care for the needs of a person's family and carers.

Hospices would specialise in palliative[120] care. This type of care aims to relieve suffering and improve the quality of life for anyone living with a serious illness. The doctors have expert training in pain management and symptom control.

A hospice care team can typically include doctors, nurses, home health aides, spiritual counsellors, social workers, volunteers, physical, occupational and speech

---

[118] *LifeBook*, www.ageuk.org.uk.

[119] 'End of Life Care', www.nhs.uk.

[120] www.palliativedoctors.org/faq.

therapists, and bereavement counsellors. It can also provide respite care.

Most hospice care can be provided in your own home. Therefore if you have discovered your illness is incurable, reaching out for the quality of care offered by a hospice is something to be done sooner rather than later. Hospice care will provide for all of a patient's medical needs related to symptom management and comfort care. This includes, among other things, providing in your own home a hospital bed, shower chair, and alternating pressure mattress. It is a wonderful way of being able to remain in your most precious and familiar surroundings with your family and friends.

Hospice care can be provided in a care home. You can also be a day patient visiting the hospice looking after you.

Hospice care is free of charge twenty-four hours a day. It is available for adults, children and young people. It can be provided at any stage of a person's illness, not just at the end of life. You can contact a hospice directly, but you will usually need a referral from your doctor or nurse.

Ways to find a local hospice

- Ask your GP or district nurse;

- Use www.nhs.uk end-of-life care and hospices search;

- Contact www.hospiceuk.org;

- Make use of the 'Find me help' service www.help.dyingmatters.org;

- www.hospiceaid.org.uk;

Useful organisations:

- www.mariecurie.org.uk – search for Hospice Care or Marie Curie Support Line;
- National Council for Palliative Care www.ncpc.org.uk;
- Sue Ryder hospices www.sueryder.org;
- videos and written interviews of people talking about planning for the future www.healthtalk.org.

Making goals, having something to look forward to, having fun

You are not dead yet; there is still time to live.

What are your thoughts? Any final desires?

There is much talk these days of bucket lists. One person I met had always wanted to experience being weightless, like an astronaut, so she learned to scuba dive. It can be as off the wall as you like, it is entirely up to you. You might have to accept the fact that some things you consider may not be possible, but have fun dreaming and choosing.

Ask yourself the very important relational questions. Whom do I love? Whom do I want to be with? Whom do I want to say thank you to?

Suggestions:

- Travel – see the Northern Lights; visit the Pyramids or the Grand Canyon; hire a canal boat and potter down a river or two.
- Sport – see a favourite team play your favourite sport; snorkel in the Great Barrier reef; ride in a hot-air

balloon; run a kilometre, a half-marathon, a marathon; learn to dance the tango; swim with dolphins.

- Arts – write that book; learn to paint/draw; knit that sweater; make that quilt; learn carpentry

- Do some charitable work.

- Friends – buy a hugely expensive bottle of wine and invite your friends; eat at a restaurant you have always wanted to; write each friend a note expressing what their friendship has meant to you.

- Family – your spouse/partner: what have they always wanted to do? Do it with them; see a family member who lives abroad; revisit the places of your life.

- Give away the things that mean so much to you, explaining why they are so important.

- Organise a party while there is still time to participate.

- Perhaps we might like to write a letter of love to each of our precious ones. A beautiful and irreplaceable parting gift.

Tim McGraw, in his wonderful song 'Live Like You Were Dying', writes the final word on bucket lists. Written in 2004 by Tim Nichols and Craig Wiseman in response to family and friends being struck by life-limiting illnesses, they noticed how in many their perspective changed. They decided to do things they had always hankered after. In some it changed them into more rounded gracious people.

Their words inspired my own, not that I have a life-limiting illness.

Why did I wait?

The sun got deeper
The green got greener
Beauty blossomed everywhere I looked.
People's faces imprinted keener
Kindness gathered, gushing like a stream
Into every crevasse.
I ran, I rode, I flew, I stilled
But most of all I danced
Inside and out
To the song of life
In all its fullness.

How does our daily life stand up in the light of eternity? Marijke Hoek,[121] a theologian and lecturer, reminds us of Etty Hillesum.[122] This brave Dutch lady supported the Jewish people in occupied Holland during the Second World War. It killed her. She wrote an inspiring thought about a spider.

> When a spider weaves a web it throws out the main threads ahead of itself and then follows it. The main thread in my life is way ahead of me in another world. I'm already building that new society.

---

[121] Marijke Hoek, theologian and lecturer, *Friday Night Theology*, www.eauk.org, February 2017.
[122] Etty Hillesum, diarist and letter writer who wrote about her faith and the persecution of the Jews during the German occupation of Holland.

As God-lovers, the only way to resurrection is through death. Our future hope is vast in relation to our time on this earth. It is said that we take nothing with us when we die. The knowledge of God we have acquired on earth, the love we have given and received in our relationships: this is what we take with us. These things are eternal. Like the spider, part of me already resides in and has taken hold of what God has promised me.

Finale

The Bible's book of Job is about a man of great wealth, but even more importantly a man of supreme character, who loved and served God his whole life. This he outworked in his care for the poor, for the dispossessed, the widow and the orphan and his generous contribution into the community in which he lived. If Job spoke, people listened and recognised his wisdom. Yet this man, over a period of days, lost everything. All his immense quantity of flocks and herds were stolen. His servants were killed. His ten children died in a freak accident. His mental and emotional agony must have been total. Finally his entire body became diseased from head to toe. His wife's response was, 'Curse God and die!' (Job 2:9).

Job refused. He believed God was in charge of all things. He understood his agony was nothing to do with any judgement for his wrongdoing. He had lived a faithful and upright life. Bad things happen to good people. Bad people often seem to flourish. One day God will put all this right.

In the midst of his torment, Job utters the sublime words of faith which we recognise from Handel's *Messiah*. In uttering these words Job glimpses his future hope.

I know that my Redeemer lives,
and that in the end he will stand upon the earth.
And after my skin has been destroyed,
yet in my flesh I will see God.
Job 19:25–26

Wherever you are on your journey, I pray that you find such faith as Job, despite all the pain of the present. You are beloved by God, and I leave you with a magnificent psalm. The words in italics are mine. May it fill you with hope.

Psalm 23

The LORD is my shepherd,
The Lord is my guide, my healer and my protector
I shall not be in want.
The Lord Himself is my complete fulfilment
He makes me lie down in green pastures,
He brings me to an ever-present place of rest
he leads me beside quiet waters,
He refreshes me, restores me, renews me
he restores my soul.
He helps me turn back and reclaim all I have lost
He guides me in paths of righteousness
He shows me what is right and helps me to walk with purpose
for his name's sake.
Because He has promised to love me
Even though I walk through the valley of the shadow of death,
Whatever crises I face

I will fear no evil,
I choose to respond not with fear but with faith
for you are with me;
Only because You are my friend and walk alongside me
your rod and your staff, they comfort me.
Your constant attention to the detail of my life,
and Your willingness to fight for me
bring me security
You prepare a table before me in the presence of my
enemies.
I will feast on You in the midst of all that threatens
to overwhelm me
You anoint my head with oil;
You equip me and honour me
my cup overflows.
I have access to all I need
Surely goodness and love will follow me all the days of
my life,
Your promised love pursues me daily without fail
and I will dwell in the house of the LORD for ever.
You will be the constant focus of my life now and
for evermore.

We do not approach death uncertain whether we are
worthy of eternal life. We believe in Jesus, who is the
only worthy One, and we are safe in him.
Tim Keller[123]

---

[123] Keller, *Making Sense of God*, p. 174.

My prayer for you

May the God who sees you, who knows you by name,
who loves you beyond measure,
who suffered for you, and suffers still alongside you, fill
you with His peace.
May His joy rise within you.
May His hope fill your eyes.
May His love enfold you.
May you receive His promises[124] you will not die alone,
and there is an eternal
place prepared for you.
Amen

As I finish this book I wait for news on my son and daughter-in-law's baby who is having an operation on this very day. He now weighs about 6lbs. Yesterday when he left our house to go into hospital held in my son's arms, I called his name. He turned and looked at me full in the face and listened intently while I spoke to him. He gave me a smile and then they left.

Today I howled in prayer for the mercy of God. When the call came in the evening that he was safe in his parents' arms, my husband and I celebrated. There are no guarantees in this life. Although I believe with my whole heart that God is good all the time, tough, terrible and painful things happen. Sometimes we will have to wait

---

[124] Matthew 28:20: 'I am with you each and every day until the end of the age' (ISV).

until we go through our own portal in order to be reunited.
Love is never wasted.

Now is your time of grief, but I will see you again and
you will rejoice, and no one will take away your joy.
John 16:22

APPENDIX 1
To-do list when someone dies[125]

When someone close dies, especially if you are the next of kin and/or an executor and/or attorney, you are usually in shock, yet there are plenty of practical tasks. So here's a suggested list of things that you may need to do with the great help of my friend Helen Calder.

You may find it helpful to keep a 'to-do' list in a notebook or on your computer or smartphone.

The day of the death

- Try to give yourself a bit of space and remember to eat and drink, even if you don't feel like it; you'll need the energy.

- If someone dies at home, contact the doctor to certify death. The hospital, hospice or nursing home will arrange this where appropriate.

- Check the death does not have to be reported to the coroner, as this could affect burial time.

---

[125] See also *When Someone Dies* Age UK booklet, www.ageuk.org.uk. Search: When Someone Dies (PDF, 365 KB). 'What to Do after Someone Dies', www.gov.uk/after-a-death.

- If someone dies at home, contact a funeral director to collect the body. Hopefully, details will be in place. You will need to confirm once the doctor has visited, as they cannot collect until death is certified. The hospital, hospice or nursing home may arrange this where appropriate, but do check. You may also choose to give the funeral director some clothes for the body for the coffin. NB: Once the funeral director collects the body, you are incurring costs so you may want to ask for an estimate when you make the initial call (though this may not feel important at the time).

- Start to let other people know face to face/by phone/by email/by text/by letter:

  o family/relatives;

  o close friends;

  o employer;

  o neighbours;

  o wider circle of friends (you can usually do this once funeral arrangements have been made.

- Do accept offers of help. The list of names to be contacted plus contact details could be something already in place.

Next day

- Collect the death certificate, usually from the GP or hospital.

- Arrange to register the death with the Registrar's Office (you need the death certificate to do this). The registrar will give you copies of the registration. (You are likely to need at least five and you may need ten plus. Every cancellation required will ask for proof of death. It is cheaper to do all copies at the time.) Collect a green form to give to the funeral director. Also collect a 'Tell us once' form for notifications after the funeral.

- Arrange appointment with funeral director/burial director to make or implement the burial/cremation arrangements. If a natural burial, body preparation must fulfil the natural burial requirements (ie not be embalmed).

- Contact the solicitor/bank who holds the will or whoever has a copy.

- You may be the sole executor. If not, contact the executors of the will if they are known to you. All the arrangements can then be shared. Say yes to any help offered.

Before the funeral

Meet with funeral director and/or church minister. Some of the things they may ask include (it may help to have advance notice of this):

- Date and location preferred for funeral/cremation/burial/thanksgiving service.

- Where ashes will be placed. This could be at the crematorium or at the funeral directors, if you want to collect the ashes for scattering or placing elsewhere.

- Alternatively, where the burial will take place.

- Person to take service(s).

- Type of coffin and lining – if natural burial, this must be biodegradable.

- Casket, if required for ashes.

- Cars, if required for relatives.

- Other requirements, eg horse-drawn carriage coffin, release of doves.

- Music, hymns, songs, readings, tribute, speaker for service.

- Details of organist or other musicians for service(s).

- A display of photographs at the services, plus/or digital photographs.

- A Book of Remembrance at the service to record attendance and/or for people to write comments in.

- The funeral director to place a death announcement in any local or national newspapers. Or do this yourself.

- Check/arrange PA system, stewards and car-park attendant for any church service(s).

- Arrange 'in memory' gifts to be given to a favourite charity if this is preferred to flowers.

- Arrange flowers for funeral – coffin, church etc – with florist. Agree what happens to the flowers after the service(s).

- Consider detailed format and content of service(s).

- Ask people you'd like to do any readings, prayers and tributes at service(s).

- Arrange catering for any reception/meal/drinks/tea after service(s).

- Arrange printing of any orders of service. Perhaps include some photos of the person, a short biography, details of any gifts 'in memory'.

- Notify funeral/cremation/thanksgiving service arrangements to:

  o family/relatives;

  o close friends;

  o employer;

  o neighbours;

  o wider circle of friends (you can usually do this once funeral arrangements have been made;

  o newspaper – a good way to inform the person's local community, if appropriate.

A Christmas card list or address book is a good source of information regarding whom to inform.

Finance

Why not find a way to have access to cash prior to the death, in order that these things can be paid for? For example, set up a joint account with your relative.

- Funeral director (if a solicitor is handling probate/will, it might be possible for them to settle the invoice from the proceeds of the estate);
- Church minister (the funeral director may offer to handle this);
- Organist (the funeral director may offer to handle this);
- Florist;
- Caterer.

After the funeral

Notify:

- Solicitor if not already done;
- Banks and building societies;
- Department for Work & Pensions;
- Use 'Tell us once' form provided by the registrar. You can do this by phone or online.

Collect belongings/furniture from hospital, hospice or nursing home where relevant.

NB: Care home or nursing home final fees are usually dependant on when you clear the room.

Thank-you/appreciation notes

- Minister;
- Organist/musicians if personally known and booked direct;
- People who do readings, tributes in service(s);
- People who have particularly helped and supported you.

Solicitor/bank holding the will

This may cover the contents of the will and whether you want the solicitor/bank to arrange probate (cost typically £750 to £1,500 dependent on where in the country they are), or to do the work in winding up the estate on behalf of the executors (cost typically 2 per cent of gross estate, including probate). If you want the solicitor/bank to do probate or the whole winding up of estate, it helps to have a list of the person's assets, ie bank and building society accounts, investments, property, valuable jewellery, etc. You will be asked to provide latest bank statements and share certificates (if appropriate).

Other suggestions

Other people are often keen to help but don't always know how. Some suggestions are outlined below – they may:

- Accompany you on visits, eg to collect death certificate; to see registrar, funeral director or minister;

- Help with notifications, funeral and thanksgiving arrangements;

- Make meals for you;

- Invite you for meals;

- Have a coffee or go for a walk with you;

- Do some shopping;

- Spend time listening to you;

- Help with clearing hospice or care home room swiftly;

- Help with house clearance after the funeral.

NB: You may want to talk about the person who has died, but others avoid the subject for fear of causing upset. Take the initiative in mentioning the deceased.

Reading all the above, you will realise how important it is to talk about and plan these things in advance. In the midst of your shock and grief, being hijacked by innumerable questions and decisions is challenging.

A folder containing all the information pertaining to a person's life as they approach their end of life allows peace of mind for both the person dying and the person/people who will then take responsibility afterwards. It might contain the following information:

- A funeral plan already in place;

- A funeral director or national firm, if that is required;

- The order of service or contents of the funeral/service of thanksgiving etc, with suggestions as to contributors;

- Details of where the will is held, with names and contact numbers for the executors;

- Name of the solicitor;

- List of contacts' names and addresses/email;

- A list of assets: property, bank accounts, investments, jewellery, etc;

- Passwords to any electronic assets;

- Passwords to all online assets – prior to death is helpful;

- Details of Advance Decision;

- Details of Lasting Power of Attorney for finance and/or health and welfare, with names and contact details of attorneys.

APPENDIX 2
Choosing a care home or nursing home

This can be a challenging task, particularly if you have a relative who is reluctant to leave their own home.

The Care Quality Commission (CQC)[126] website is a great place to start. You can search by postcode. It may be prudent to consider places which have 'outstanding' and 'good' ratings for everything. If somewhere near has lower ratings, ask questions why the rating wasn't so good. Check what the latest CQC report actually says.

Things to consider include:

1. Location, in terms of convenience for the most frequent visitors.

2. CQC rating.

3. Fees – what's included:

   - What level of care does that include?

   - Are there extras?

   - What if the level of care required is reduced or increased? How is that assessed?

---

[126] Care Quality Commission, www.cqc.org.uk.

4. The ambience of the home:

    •   Is it friendly and welcoming?

    •   How does it compare to homes already visited (but not in the right location)?

5. Does it have a fresh, clean smell?

6. How clean are the bedrooms and communal rooms? Look under the beds and in the corners of the bathroom floor.

7. What are the residents' rooms and communal rooms like? In the communal lounges, is the seating in small groups or one big circle facing a communal TV? The former is infinitely preferable.

8. Check precisely which rooms they are offering you.

    •   Does the preferred room have en suite facilities? A shower and toilet is important, particularly if incontinence becomes an issue. An older person is more likely to need assistance with a bath so an en suite bath becomes less important than a shower. A seat in the shower is helpful.

    •   Is there a view from the room? Important if someone becomes bedbound or room-bound.

    •   Is all furniture provided, or can a resident have some/all of their own furniture?

    •   Are hospital-style beds provided or available when required? Should a hospice provide care later, a hospital bed will be provided.

- Check personal pictures, ornaments etc are allowed.

- Are there phones in residents' rooms? If not, can they be installed? Check charges for installation, line rental and call charges (which may be part of the home's telephone contract). There are good mobile phones for the elderly available. Is there Wi-Fi?

- Are there emergency call buttons in residents' rooms?

9. Are there gardens and outside space where residents can sit?

10. Ask to see a menu, and go in the dining room when residents are eating.

11. Check arrangements if a resident would prefer to eat in their room.

12. What activities and outings are offered?

13. What level of medical care is available on site, eg qualified nurses: during the day, twenty-four hours? Hospice care can be implemented in the care home as end of life approaches.

14. What arrangements are there for GP visits to the home, or for taking residents to the GP?

15. What is the situation if a resident needs to go to outpatients (some homes charge extra for this)?

16. Does the home provide wheelchairs, or would you need to supply your own?

17. How much parking is there for visitors, and how easy is it to collect a resident from the front door?

18. How do the staff present? How do they treat residents? How do they treat you? What is morale like? How accessible is the manager/matron for a conversation?

19. Ask to speak to a family member of a current resident and to a current resident, preferably without being accompanied by a member of staff.

20. If you have shortlisted homes after visiting, have a good look at the contract, especially the notice period if someone dies (extra charges can be incurred). Sometimes it's until you move out all belongings, for some it's four weeks. Also, how much of the fee is payable if the resident is admitted to hospital?

21. Is the home eligible for financial contributions from the NHS or social services?

22. Check if the resident will get follow-up nursing care when discharged from hospital. It is not means-tested but there is a scoring exercise to see what level of ongoing nursing will be required.

APPENDIX 3
Visiting activities

Many people visiting relatives, friends or neighbours are unsure what to do and say when visiting the sick, or those with dementia.

Some suggestions:

1. Bring a newspaper or magazine (preferably tabloid-size for ease) and look at it together.

2. Think of an amusing anecdote to recount of something that's happened since your last visit.

3. Take flowers and encourage the person you're visiting to arrange them in a vase, assisting as necessary. Talk about the names and colours of the flowers.

4. Autumn leaves are also something from outdoors that can be of interest.

5. Do soothing, simple things related to a hobby the person has/had – stamp album, sewing, crochet, knitting, gardening (eg plant a bulb in a pot).

6. Take a favourite food (subject to medical restrictions). Chocolate Buttons are great for those experiencing swallowing difficulty as they melt in the mouth. Ice cream brought in a cool bag can be popular.

7. Get a tea or coffee or cold drink for you both to have together.

8. Visit at a meal-time and sit with the person. Assist them to eat if helpful.

9. Read to the person. Perhaps a book where you can read a chapter each time you visit.

10. Look at a picture or coffee-table-type book together, eg on the royal family, countryside, buildings, countries they may have visited, a favourite artist.

11. Listen to an audio book together.

12. Look at pictures of family, friends, favourite places, holidays, old photos from earlier years.

13. Wedding photos are often particularly special, and you may be able to pick out relatives and friends.

14. Look at recent letters and cards that have been sent, and read the messages out.

15. Read letters or cards that may have been sent in the past, or a diary.

16. A holiday journal and looking at the relevant holiday photos can be particularly fun, recounting the memories.

17. Play some favourite music: classical, pop or spiritual. Music seems to resonate well with people with dementia, and often makes them more alert and communicative.

18. Do something devotional:

- Read a Bible passage: a favourite, something encouraging or calming (the Psalms are particularly good);

- Offer to sing a hymn or spiritual song: they may like to join in;

- Play a hymn on a Kindle or similar device;

- Read hymns and ask them to choose their favourites;

- Offer to pray for the person;

- Pray a blessing over them;

- Combine these into a little service;

- Break bread with them.

19. Watch a TV programme together, especially something they enjoy, eg sport, *Songs of Praise*, a serial.

20. Listen to a brief radio programme together. You could use BBC 'Listen Again' for one previously broadcast.

21. Offer to wipe their face with a warm, damp flannel (take a flannel and towel with you).

22. Offer a manicure, hand massage or nail painting (take a flannel, towel, nail clippers, nail varnish, varnish remover and hand cream with you).

23. Rub body lotion gently into arms or legs (having sought permission first!).

24. Hold a hand or stroke a hand, arm or brow. Touch can be very soothing and comforting.

25. Use your mobile to phone a friend. Even if the person can't speak, hearing a familiar voice will be an encouragement. Using speaker phone may help so you can both hear the conversation.

26. Skype a relative or friend who lives at a distance so they can see them.

27. Go and sit somewhere together where you can watch the world go by: near an entrance or communal area.

28. Go for a wheelchair ride:

    - round the building;

    - in the grounds/garden;

    - to the care home's or hospital's café or communal lounge.

29. Take them out for a country drive (or even a town drive). The change of scene can be a real tonic. Talk about what you can both see.

30. Taking an audio book reader or tablet can be very useful for photos, music, books, TV shows, films etc.

Resources

Bibliography

Anastasios, Andrew, *Dying to Know* (Australia: Pilotlight / London: Hardie Grant Books, 2010)

Bereavement booklet, available at www.rcpsych.ac.uk

Brown, Brené, *The Gifts of Imperfection* (Center City, MN: Hazelden Publishing, 2010)

Carter, Marian, *Dying to Live* (London: SCM Press, 2014)

Davies, Rev Belinda, *GraveTalk* (London: Church House Publishing, 2015), www.gravetalk.org

Gawande, Atul, *Being Mortal* (London, Profile Books, 2015)

Graham, Jim, *Dying to Live* (London: Marshall Morgan & Scott, 1984)

GraveTalk Facilitators' Guide (Church House Publishing, 2015)

Keller, Tim, *Making Sense of God* (New York: Viking, 2016)

Kübler-Ross, Elisabeth MD, *On Death & Dying* (New York: Scribner, 2014)

Living with Death and Dying, Open University, www.open.edu (free course)

Morse, Louise, *What Matters in the End* (London: Pilgrims' Friend Society, 2016), www.pilgrimsfriend.org.uk

Solomon, Sheldon; Greenberg, Jeff; Pyszczynski, Tom, *The Worm at the Core* (London: Penguin Books, 2016)

When Someone Dies booklet. Age UK, available www.ageuk.org.uk/moneymatters

Wienrich, Stephanie and Speyer, Josefine (editors), *The Natural Death Handbook* (London: Rider Books, 2003)

Wright, Tom, *Revelation for Everyone* (London: SPCK, 2011)

Wright, Tom, *Surprised by Hope* (London: SPCK, 2012)

Wyatt, John, *Matters of Life & Death* (Leicester: IVP, 2012)

Websites

(all current, March 2017)

Funerals

- The cost of dying, www.sunlife.co.uk
- Fair Funerals Campaign,
- The Royal London National Funeral Cost Index Report 2016, www.royallondon.com
- National Association of Funeral Directors, www.nafd.org.uk
- National Society of Allied and Independent Funeral Directors, www.saif.org.uk

Other websites

- Dying Matters, www.dyingmatters.org

- Let's Have Dinner and Talk About Death,
  www.facebook.com/LetsHaveDinnerandTalkAboutDeath
  @LetsHaveDinnerandTalkAboutDeath

- Ruby Care Foundation, www.rubycare.org

- Patients First Network, www.spuc.org.uk

- Natural Death Centre, www.naturaldeath.org.uk

- Hospice UK, www.hospiceaid.org.uk

- Sue Ryder, www.sueryder.org

- Make a Wish Foundation (for children), www.make-a-wish.org.uk

- Just Visiting, www.justvisiting.com (the sharing
  network for caring people. Allows you to register,
  create a room, invite friends and family to visit and
  begin posting messages.)

- Dreamflight, www.dreamflight.org (to send seriously
  ill children on the holiday of a lifetime)

- Marie Curie Cancer Care, www.mariecurie.org.uk

- Acorns Children's Hospice Trust, www.acorns.org.uk
  (care and support for children and their families)

- UKHCA – UK Home Care Association,
  www.ukhca.co.uk

- Willow Foundation, www.willowfoundation.org.uk
  (brings special days to those between sixteen and
  forty)

- Macmillan Cancer Support, www.macmillan.org.uk

- Together for Short Lives, www.togetherforshortlives.org.uk (a children's palliative care charity)

- The National Council for Palliative Care, www.ncpc.org.uk (umbrella organisation for all providing, commissioning and using hospice and palliative care services in UK)

- Bereaved Parent Support, www.careforthefamily.org.uk

- INQUEST, www.inquest.org.uk (charity providing specialist and comprehensive advice on contentious deaths and their investigation)

- Winston's Wish www.winstonswish.org (supports young people who have experienced bereavement)

- Cruse Bereavement Care, www.cruse.org.uk

- Child Bereavement UK, www.childbereavementuk.org (charity for bereaved young people)

- Compassion in Dying, www.compassionindying.org.uk

- The Art of Dying Well, www.artofdyingwell.org

- Age UK, www.ageuk.org.uk

- Samaritans, www.samaritans.org

- Office of the Public Guardian, www.gov.uk/government/organisations/office-of-the-public-guardian

- London Friend LGBT Bereavement Help, www.londonfriend.org.uk

- Citizens Advice, www.citizensadvice.org.uk

- Association of Christian Counsellors, http://www.acc-uk.org

- www.healthtalk.org

- www.counselling-directory.org.uk

- www.griefwords.com

- www.rcpsych.ac.uk

- www.deathisnotdying.com

- www.Ata**Loss**.org

1 Cor 15:6

I just realised that dying was not actually about me, it
was about
Those around me; it was about their feelings, it was about
their comfort,
It was about their coping, their knowing that I loved
them,
And it was leaving nothing unsaid.
Maxine Edginton[127]

[127] Maxine Edginton died of cancer in 2005. She co-wrote the single 'We Laughed' with Billy Bragg as part of the Rosetta Life Project, www.rosettalife.org.

For more information about the author and her work, please visit her website: www.annclifford.co.uk.

Alternatively, connect with Ann on social media:
Twitter: @1AnnClifford
Facebook.com/TimetoLiveAC/

CT Scan — xray radiation
MRI " imaging
benign cyst — bag oj fluid
Satsuma size —
drained 3rd — resection 6/12 —

UKLB3OHE a checkout
Hair + Energy —